Miracle Makeo

with the

Garden Guru

ANTONY HENN

BBC BOOKS

Acknowledgements

My first love as a boy was always wild animals and birds and I always planned to be a gamekeeper in Kenya. I only began to develop an interest in plants and gardening whilst helping my father out at the family nursery in my school holidays. His enthusiasm was infectious and even though I resisted at first, I too was soon hooked.
A big thank you to Tessa Finch and Alex Frazer at Pebble Mill for giving me the opportunity to share my love of nature and design with the
Good Morning . . . audience.
Thanks must also go to Jane Root and Alex Graham at Wall to Wall Television, who asked me to present the series and write the book without ever doubting my capabilities.
My ice-cool producer Gavin Rota, and whiz-kid researcher Louise Jones, always behaved like true professionals throughout the series, no matter how tough things got. They were also great fun to work with, as were all the talented crew who were never afraid to muck in and get their hands dirty.
My friend and colleague, Russell Jeffery has worked hard with me to create the wonderful gardens for the TV series. His skill and determination to do the job right have been invaluable.
Finally, many thanks to Rosanne Hunt who has been a tower of strength and supported me throughout the past year.

This book is published to accompany the *Garden Guru* series which is part of *Good Morning . . . with Anne and Nick*. The *Garden Guru* is produced for the BBC by Wall to Wall Television Limited.

Published by BBC Books,
an imprint of BBC Worldwide Publishing.
BBC Worldwide Limited
Woodlands, 80 Wood Lane
London W12 0TT

First published 1995

ISBN 0 563 37134 X

Typeset in Bembo by Ace Filmsetting Ltd, Frome
Colour reproduction by Radstock Reproductions, Midsomer Norton
Printed in Great Britain by Cambus Litho Ltd, East Kilbride
Bound in Great Britain by Hunter & Foulis Ltd, Edinburgh
Cover printed by Clays Ltd, St Ives plc

Contents

Introduction

Gardening for me has always been fun, challenging and immensely rewarding, but for the 'non-believer' who has just adopted an overgrown wilderness, it can be an absolute nightmare!

This book is different from other gardening volumes in that it sets out to demystify garden design and transformation. By following the step-by-step methods described, even the complete non-gardener will be amazed at what can be achieved. It will also be of interest to the keen but disheartened gardener who needs inspiration.

You may have a well-crafted garden for instance, but perhaps you have a very dry bank that is proving difficult, or you wish to create a pond and rockery. These and other projects are tackled in the relevant chapters.

Using existing plants and materials wherever possible is obviously cheaper and less wasteful (areas close to my heart!); merely repositioning a particular tree or shrub to create a focal point, or adding a few more ground-cover plants to form a bold group, can improve a scheme instantly, without great expense.

Materials such as old bricks and rock that could be deemed skip-worthy, can often be utilized and will add maturity and character to a new patio area for instance. (See the chapter on transforming a patio garden.)

Trees and shrubs that have got completely out of hand, may only need a serious pruning to rejuvenate them. Others may not be worth saving and advice on identification and how to attack a 'jungle' will be discussed in the chapter on the Neglected Garden. It is important not to rush into any decision on the fate of trees and shrubs in your garden before close identification and analysis; five minutes with a chainsaw can do irrevocable damage. Just think how much it would cost to replace a mature specimen shrub or rare tree, or how long it will take to grow one to that size again. Hold fire and read on.

Being sympathetic to the environment and creating a garden to be lived in, yet easily maintained, are factors discussed in each chapter.

The eight very different themes to my book involve solutions to particular problem gardens, whether it's what to grow under a large tree that casts lots of shade for instance, or the type of plants and materials suitable for a city roof garden.

Most problem areas in the garden can be approached and solved by the enthusiastic non-professional. Anything more difficult, especially involving electricity, or that might be dangerous in any way (such as fixing railing to your roof garden), should be handled by a professional.

Contained in each chapter is the garden makeover, as seen on BBC Television. Explanations on how each problem garden was transformed are given, and with the help of before and after photographs the visual metamorphosis is clearly shown.

There are a few design rules, however, which if followed, will help to achieve success more easily. Whether you're about to take on a wildlife garden, create a water feature from scratch, or are wondering what on earth to grow in a children's garden, the steps described here should help you to accomplish this.

● **Step 1** Assess the needs of the family or people living there. Children need special consideration, as do elderly folk and people with disabilities. Also important, is to consider the budget available and whether your ideas should perhaps be scaled down to suit this. Planning ahead so that certain features can be added later may be useful if funds are limited.

● **Step 2** Make a note of what is already there, what you wish to keep and how it can be utilized in the design. Spend some time getting the 'feel' of the area and use a hosepipe and bamboo canes to get ideas of shape and scale for any planned features. Note the aspect of the garden.

● **Step 3** Measure the area and draw up a simple plan of what you've got. Use a scale rule so it's easier to measure off the finished plan later. Omit undesirable objects and draw in the new design, using pencil as you are bound to change your mind many times! It's best to use tracing paper over the basic layout plan, so it's easy to see what it was like before. Keep the design simple. A to-scale plan is also invaluable when trying to work out materials and costings. The numbers of plants needed can also be more easily calculated.

chapter one

The Patio Garden

An area of paving close to the house is one of the most commonly used parts of the garden, whether it's for barbecuing, entertaining or simply relaxing in the sun. It is also the site most often viewed from the house. That's why I feel it is so important to get it right first time.

Patios are useful in any size garden. A small patio can become a courtyard garden, useful for town houses; a larger patio can 'set off' a large garden or become the outdoor room that leads to the rest of the garden.

Choosing the right material for the job is critical, as you will be spending a lot of time admiring your patio area. Take time to look at the house style and bricks used for it, to get an idea of what will look right.

Creating an area large enough for entertaining is of great importance. Imagine the space a table and a few chairs take up and the room needed to allow access for a group of merry party guests.

Even crazy paving can look superb if dressed up with suitable plants.

Pots of plants can soon dress-up an otherwise hard-looking surface and can easily be moved to create space when required. Remember that extending it later may look obvious and stand out like a sore thumb.

DESIGN

To maximize the space available, it is well worth drawing up a plan of your proposed patio area. Remember to note where the sun and shade occur and create a sitting area accordingly. Note that even in this country some patios can become too hot to sit on comfortably in summer and so a pergola may be required. The dictionary definition of a patio is 'a paved area adjoining the house' and although it is nice to be able to walk from the house onto the patio, it does not necessarily have to be adjoining. Place it further away if it will catch the sun better.

I often like to link the paved area to the garden somehow. This can be achieved by leaving spaces in the patio area where low alpines or herbs can be planted, or staggering the edges so that the grass or plants can encroach onto the patio. We put both these ideas into practice in the television makeover (page 16).

Drawing a plan will also assist in calculating the materials needed for the job. Over ordering can be expensive.

As always, I try to create something that is sympathetic to its surroundings. The same principle applies to designing a patio area: the practical needs of the owner are the first considerations whether it's for a young family or elderly people. Note that paving is far easier to maintain than well-planted borders or lawn. A large patio may therefore meet the requirements of elderly or physically disabled people.

SPECIAL FEATURES FOR PATIOS

● Patterns in the patio using old bricks or cobbles can look great. I've even seen the upturned ends of green bottles embedded in cement in a paved area! Coloured stones can be used to form an intricate mosaic which can make the whole area very personal indeed.
● Water on the patio adds life and movement to what may be a rather stark area. Even a small water feature can create a strong focal point and the sound of gurgling water is *so* therapeutic.
● Specimen plants in tubs work beautifully. This is a particularly good way of growing those whose soil requirements do not match that which is in your garden.

Important things to consider for design aspects are:

● Size: although an area may seem far too large for your potential patio, remember furniture and pots can take up a lot of space.
● Never slope the patio towards the house as rain water needs to run away from it.
● Always ensure that the damp course is at least two bricks above the level of the paving.

STYLES AND THEMES

Patio design can be formal or informal. Style of house and size of garden will influence your choice. Older character houses will lend themselves to a more formal patio, with a balustrade edging or low walls, clipped evergreen plants in ornamental containers, or 'disciplined' paving. Informality will be achieved by random-sized paving, with planting gaps.

FORMAL

If the area is large enough, you can use something quite bold visually to give a striking focal point:

● A central gazebo with seating inside will offer a place to sit in the summer. If climbing plants are grown through it, a wonderful visual impression can be made.
● Tiered water fountains are extensively used around the world in formal gardens and can be a strong feature as a centrepiece to a large patio.

- Wall-mounted water features above a painted bench with a couple of ornamental pots each side, would be a simple way to introduce formality to a smaller patio.

Formal courtyard gardens were used throughout history for relaxing and studying. Effective use can be made of herringbone brick or large natural stone slabs; pots with clipped box and yew; or a fish pool such as can be seen in Mediterranean and eastern countries where smooth marble slabs are used with long, but very narrow pools built within the patio. More suitable materials (non-slip) should be used in the UK and hardier plants such as Portuguese laurel or pittosporum would be substitutes for citrus etc.

INFORMAL

A paved area amongst shrubs in the garden can also be classed as a patio. It may be the only place to sit in the sun if the main patio is on the north side of the house, for instance. The choice of materials is enormous. Old council paving can be used and by removing the odd slab, and filling the space with stone chips or plants, a totally different and usually pleasing result can be achieved. Try-ing to utilize existing materials wherever possible will save a lot of money. Removing the odd slab along the edge of the patio can also help to create an informal effect.

Other informal aspects include:

- Rustic-style woodwork and furniture work well, natural timber suiting a more rural setting, or a house in a wooded area. Allow

moss or lichen to grow in the gaps of the paving stones.
- Thyme growing in the cracks of old York stone looks wonderfully natural and releases a delicious scent when walked over. Use a soil mix for pointing, then brush in thyme seed.
- A patio constructed of pressure-treated timber is popular in Scandinavia and America. This works well with modern houses, or old cottages in woodland areas, to link the house to the garden or surrounding area.

CHOOSING MATERIALS

To help you decide on what type of material to use for your patio, visit a good garden centre and look through some brochures – some have charts to help you calculate quantities. Some places have demonstration gardens, so you will see how the slabs and other materials look in situ.

Points to consider are:

- What use will the area be subjected to? Will a car ever need to drive over it? If so, a more substantial base will be required and perhaps hardened brick or block paving should be your choice.
- Again, who will be using it?
- Will the colour of the patio look right? Materials that are very light may look darker when wet, but in the height of the summer, can be too bright and dazzling. Break the area up with darker paving or bricks.
- Will you need professional help? Some patio materials are more complicated to lay than others.

● What can you afford? Original York stone is expensive, but artificial stone is much cheaper and can be very effective.

BLOCK PAVING

A few years ago this type of paving was highly expensive and quite up-market. Nowadays, it is far more competitive and hence you see it everywhere.

Although it can look a bit like a garage forecourt it is very useful indeed in some respects. The blocks (looking like bricks) are laid on sand over a substantial sub-base, and so can be easily removed (or replaced) if any ground work is needed in that area (e.g. cable laying or pipe repair).

I personally find that for a patio area they look far better if blended in with paving stones. This will be a bit more fiddly to achieve as they are of different thicknesses, but well worth the effort. There are many different colours to choose from – blending in with other stone should not be difficult.

Another plus-point for using block paving is the fact that they last indefinitely, and with the correct preparation they are actually quite easy to lay. Do not worry about a white residue (lime) which appears soon after laying as this will fade.

BRICKS

Frost-proof bricks are now being made to look as if they are many years old, with varying shades and deliberate unevenness on their surface. These look superb in a courtyard-style patio, or if the patio needs to look aged and in keeping with an old building. The bricks can also be used to build low raised beds enclosing the area. Plants can be planted in the spaces between, if two low walls 40 cm (16 in) apart are built.

Laying a patio of bricks, whether it be herringbone or basket-weave style, is not easy. If you are of a practical nature, I'm sure with initial guidance it can be accomplished. If not, then call in a skilled person as these bricks are expensive and once spoiled by stray cement, are ruined. Do not use normal house bricks which will break up in frost.

You will need a sub-base followed by a sand and cement base. Careful pointing-up of each brick with sand and cement (the depth of the sub-base will vary depending on the usage) is time-consuming, and fiddly, but the end result can be very stylish in the right setting.

COBBLES

There are two types of cobbles: large, rounded pebbles used in water features and displays, or square-edged granite setts, as used in cobbled streets. Both are very impressive in their own right, but for a whole patio area, I find them too uneven and difficult to walk and relax on.

Rounded 'cobbles' work well as a decorative feature amongst a main area of smoother slabs or bricks. Make circular patterns of cobbles embedded in concrete or fill in a space of a missing slab such as we did in the makeover garden (page 16).

Granite 'cobbles' or setts, are a traditional material. Manufactured setts are now available and look very effective. The surface is much more even and the setts are much less thick, hence easier to lay. Attractive patterns can also be achieved, and bold circles can be useful to highlight a focal point on the patio.

Granite setts give a very relaxed feel and work brilliantly here as a seating area amongst informal plants and shrubs.

CONCRETE

Although probably the cheapest and the easiest material to lay, it is certainly not the most attractive. Coloured non-fading dyes are available to liven up the otherwise dull concrete; also exterior stone paints are often used.

If speed and budget are of the essence, then concrete will do the job satisfactorily. My advice

would be to make sure that it is laid well below the damp course (at least three to four bricks), so that paving, or another more attractive material, can be laid on top at a later date, giving the new patio a very solid base. Always leave regular expansion joints to prevent cracking.

Specialist firms now work exclusively with concrete, using moulds of different textures to leave an imprint (resembling cobbles or block paving for example) on the surface. The pattern needs to be done well, otherwise it won't fool anyone.

If opting for this product, always ask for references before agreeing to any work, to ensure that the company is reputable.

CRAZY PAVING

This used to be a cheap alternative to conventional paving, but due to higher labour charges, it is now becoming quite an expensive choice. However, if you are of a practical nature, why not tackle it yourself?

A well-laid crazy paving patio can look very attractive even though they were more fashionable in the 1970s. York crazy paving in my opinion looks far superior to broken paving slabs, but is obviously much more costly.

PAVING STONES

This is the most popular means of creating a patio. Prices range from very cheap, smooth, grey slabs, to imitation York, nearly as costly as the genuine article. The advantage in using the imitation ones, however, is that because the slabs are much thinner and more regimental than the real thing, which can vary in thickness from 5–9 cm (2–3.5 in), laying becomes much easier. Natural York paving will probably need laying by a professional because of its unevenness.

Bright colours were very popular in the 1970s, but now a more subtle look is favoured. Non-slip paving is normally recommended, but the disadvantage is that the 'pitted' surface collects dirt and algae growth more easily. Uneven, natural effect paving may look good, but may be difficult for elderly people to walk on.

Wavy-edged paving as used in the TV makeover garden (page 16) gives a totally different effect than straight-edged slabs. They need more careful pointing-up, but create a very informal impression. Varying sizes are often preferred to slabs of all the same dimension. Take care when laying irregular sizes not to end up with long, unbroken lines as this will look wrong.

Some paving slabs can be butted-up together when laid, excluding a space between them for pointing. For a formal design this works well and is also easier from a maintenance point of view as weeds and moss cannot establish themselves.

RESIN-BONDED AGGREGATE

This is becoming increasingly more popular as a surface for patios and paths. The technique involves mixing the resin with fine stones, then spreading it evenly over a hardened concrete base. This forms a very durable, long-lasting and decorative surface which is virtually non-slip. Specialist firms are generally used to apply this material as the work is highly skilled and the preparation of the base critical. A choice of stone aggregate will give the colour required and particle sizes will determine the final texture.

Resin-bonded aggregate is especially useful if you already have a solid, concrete surface. This may be too close to the damp course to allow paving or bricks to be laid on top, but the resin aggregate is laid a mere 2–3 cm (½–1 in) thick and so is ideal.

TILES

Exterior tiles look excellent in a formal design but are expensive. Make sure they are the exterior non-slip type, as most are extremely smooth. Tiles are not designed to take heavy traffic as they are quite thin, but a small area could be considered.

Tiles are laid using a special tile cement which is applied to a level concrete base. Again the laying is quite tricky, so a skilled person may be required.

Terracotta tiles are my favourite. They are thicker than most tiles, but have a slightly irregular surface and thus are a bit more fiddly to lay. A warm Mediterranean feel can be created, and a few terracotta pots with suitable plants such as bay and lavender will complete the scene.

TIMBER DECKING

Wood is a wonderful material to use for your patio area. Slight gaps between the planks can help prevent the 'ice-rink syndrome'. Take care in winter with algal growth.

Wooden tiles can be purchased from many garden centres. They will last at least 15–20 years! They look great in small gardens and I have never slipped on my wooden patio since it was constructed many years ago. These tiles have many advantages: they are lightweight, they heat up quickly in the sun and are very easy to lay. All you need is a solid level base: then simply lay them down and contain the sides to stop sideways movement. If you move house, you can simply pick them up and take them with you.

TIPS ON BUILDING THE PATIO

- Never build a patio on an unstable base. Prepare the area well before laying the surface.
- Never build a patio above the damp course (usually noticeable as a dark line in the mortar between the bricks), or rising damp will be a problem.
- Always use a spirit level and short pegs to check you have allowed sufficient depth for the base, sand and cement, and paving to end up below the damp course.
- Very dirty paving stones and bricks can be easily cleaned using a pressure sprayer, which can be hired for a few hours.
- Some long-lasting weedkillers can keep a paving area weed-free all season.
- A simple brick edge can really finish off a new or existing patio and improve its look enormously.
- If matching-up to an existing area, check that the new slabs are exactly the same size as the old, because imperial and metric sizes are different.

- Sharp sand and cement is best used under the slabs or bricks, and a finer sand and cement is best used for pointing-up. Always mix together dry and only add water when both are thoroughly mixed together.
- Concreting and cementing is best avoided in frosty weather.
- Never make the pointing mix too wet as it can stain paving.
- Sand-only slab bases may eventually become unstable with rain and soil movement, so unevenness may result. This can be useful for a short-term project: the patio material can be easily taken up and re-used.
- For cobbles, setts, concrete, crazy paving, paving stones and resin-bonded aggregate, depth of sub-base should be 50–80 mm (2–3 in) of compacted hoggin or hardcore, plus 50–80 mm (2–3 in) of sand and cement for the base. For tiles these figures are 50–80 mm (2–3 in) of concrete and 10–20 mm (½–1 in) tile cement.

PLANTINGS FOR PATIOS

Different plants will be needed depending on whether the patio is in full sun or semi-shade. Some good ideas may be gleaned from other chapters such as The Roof Garden (page 107) or The Shady Garden (page 35). You will probably want a few container plants – remember these will need feeding and watering regularly. There is a lot of fun to be had in changing the tubs from season to season. Plant tub-bound shrubs into the garden when they look a bit unhappy or are getting too large, to rejuvenate them. My favourites are listed below.

- *Buxus sempervirens* (box). Evergreen; can be clipped to any shape or size.
- *Choisya ternata* 'Sundance' (Mexican orange blossom). Evergreen; white, citrus-like flowers and golden foliage; sun or semi-shade; 90 × 90 cm (3 × 3 ft) in 5 years.
- Cistus (rock rose). Evergreen; poppy-like flowers in early summer; sun and well-drained soil; *C.* × *purpureus* grows to 90 × 90 cm (3 × 3 ft) in 5 years.

- Conifers (dwarf). Evergreen; many suitable; (see page 28–9). Varieties in various sizes available from garden centres (see also page 116).
- Fuchsias. Ideal in pots on the patio, particularly the trailing or standard varieties, but they need to be out of frost for winter except for the hardy varieties.
- Hebes. Evergreen; smaller-leaved varieties are generally hardier; some are flat-growing like *H. pinguifolia* 'Pagei' or dome-shaped like *H.* 'Red Edge'; 45 × 50 cm (18 × 20 in) in 5 years.
- Pieris (lily-of-the-valley bush) (see page 43).

- Patio roses. Long flowering period through summer; 45 × 45 cm (18 × 18 in). Prune hard in spring.
- Penstemons. Flower from mid-summer to winter; various colours. Prune in spring.
- Yucca. Evergreen; spiky leaves with tall flower spikes in late summer; good specimen plant.

Use only frost-proof bricks for paths and patios. These mixed shades give the impression of maturity and have great character.

The Patio

Paul and Sheila had recently moved in to a new bungalow. The building of it had left the garden in a bit of a state; a patio area would be ideal and useful. The design brief included a water feature and seating area. Tubs and plants would make the whole area blend in with the garden.

Design

Shape and size of the patio were determined first. We then marked up the area with pegs. An L-shaped patio was decided on, to run along the two house walls at 90 degrees to each other. One section would be wider than the other, as it caught more of the sun. The water feature was set in the corner position as that particular spot was clearly visible from the door and all the windows.

Bradstone Weatherdale paving was chosen for this patio, because its wavy edge and natural-looking surface would give the area a rural and informal look.

Ordinary planters and tubs seemed too un-imaginative; old, second-hand containers seemed a more interesting alternative. Suitable shrubs and conifers were used to add life and colour, but nothing was chosen that would grow too large.

Not the ideal place to relax and entertain!

Materials
120 × 45 × 45 cm (18 × 18 in) Bradstone Weatherdale slabs
2 cubic metres (just over 2 sq. yd) ballast
2 cubic metres (just over 2 sq. yd) sharp sand
10 × 50 kg (1 cwt) bags cement
3 × 25 kg (55 lb) bags of rounded pebbles
1 × 25 kg (55 lb) bag of red stone chippings
4 tin containers
2 clay drainage pipes
2 bags of compost
1 water feature

Step-by-step

1 **The base** As the area had already been pegged-out, it took only an hour for the JCB digger to level the ground to the right depth for the concrete base. With only two days for filming and completion, digging out by hand would have taken too long.

When we were sure that the finished paving level would be well below the damp course, a cement mixer was used to mix the ballast (gravel and sand) with the cement at a ratio of 8 to 1. The mix was spread evenly over the compressed soil surface to form our concrete base. (Hoggin or hardcore is often used under the concrete if the soil is unstable or soft.) The concrete base was left to harden overnight and was checked for levels while spreading.

2 **Laying the paving** The paving stones were all 45 × 45 cm (1½ × 1½ ft) but as this type of slab varies in thickness it had to be laid with care.

Sharp sand and cement were mixed at a 6 to 1 ratio and spread onto the hardened concrete base under each slab. A spirit level and the handle of a small mallet were used to get the levels right and to firm each paving stone down. Pointing was only done once all the slabs had bonded with the drying sand and cement.

Pointing involved filling in the gaps between the paving stones with a sand and cement mix using a narrow tool to smooth down the surface. Visually it looks better if the pointing lies just below the paving surface,

especially in this case because the edges of the slabs were attractively wavy and showed up nicely.

Three of the slabs were left out and one space was filled with rounded pebbles. The other was used as a mini-herb planter with sage and thyme, etc., and the last gap was filled with red stone chippings to link in with the red brick house. The edge of the patio was made more interesting by excluding the odd slab and filling with a dwarf shrub or conifer.

3 **Water feature** A small, recycling water unit was chosen as the focal point. A 60 cm (2 ft) diameter shallow, concrete dish was used to contain a small electrical pump which was covered by rounded 'cobbles'.

The cable had been buried under the patio earlier and fitted to an RCD unit at the mains in the garage. This safety measure is essential when using water and electricity in the garden.

When switched on, the pump produced a small jet of water through the 'cobbles' which looked just right and made a very restful and relaxing sound.

4 **Beds and planters** Alongside the patio, a narrow border was dug over and prepared for planting. We used dwarf conifers and flowering shrubs to give an evergreen structure.

Sheila bought some lovely old tin buckets and tubs from a local junk shop which looked terrific once planted up with hardy fuchsias. A couple of old clay drainage pipes were also used as original planters which gave height to the border and a fun talking point.

PLANTS USED FOR THE TV GARDEN

In containers

- 1 × *Thuja occidentalis* 'Rheingold' (see page 116)
- 2 × *Fuchsia* 'Tom Thumb'
- 1 × *Phlomis fruticosa* (Jerusalem sage). Silvery green leaves with yellow flowers; tolerant of dry soil in sun; 90 × 90 cm (3 × 3 ft) in 5 years; prune in spring.
- 1 × *Clematis* 'Jackmanii'. Vigorous climber with huge, deep purple flowers over long period; 3 × 1 m (10 × 3 ft) in 5 years.

In paving spaces

- 3 × thyme
- 1 × hyssop
- 3 × sage

Alongside

- 1 × *Hebe* 'Marjorie'
- 1 × *Hebe* 'Mrs Winder'
- 1 × *Chamaecyparis lawsoniana* 'Columnaris Glauca'. Blue-grey foliage; narrow, upright habit; 2 m × 40 cm (6 ft × 16 in) in 5 years.
- 3 × *Santolina incana* (see page 74)
- 3 × *Phlomis fruticosa*
- 1 × *Ceanothus* 'Topaz'. Deciduous; bright blue flowers in mid- to late summer; tolerant of dry soil in full sun; prune hard in spring; 1.2 × 1.2 m (4 × 4 ft) in 5 years.
- 3 × *Euonymus fortunei* 'Emerald Gaiety' (see page 44)
- 3 × *Potentilla fruticosa* 'Tilford Cream' (see page 28)

ABOVE *Hardy fuchsias are excellent container plants. This old tub adds a bit of fun.*

ABOVE *Areas of planting soften a paving area. Herbs or alpines are ideal here.*

OPPOSITE *Always leave plenty of room for access and entertaining. Using different materials in place of the odd slab adds interest.*

chapter two

The Rock Garden

In many gardens I have visited in the last few years, someone has attempted (usually unsuccessfully) to create a rockery somewhere. The result I usually refer to as 'CBS' or the 'currant bun syndrome'! This looks like a heap of earth with a number of rocks thrown at it, with no design concept or any idea what the final rockery is supposed to look like. A mass of so-called 'dwarf conifers' are crammed onto these 'rockeries', which in about four years (if they survive that long) will have totally outgrown their space.

Rocks are not cheap, so should not be wasted on poorly planned schemes. With a bit of thought and flair, an impressive rock garden can be achieved by following a few basic design principles and equally as important, by choosing the right plants for the job.

Most people want a rockery in order to enjoy the many and varied alpine plants that will grow in this country. In a smaller garden, these plants can still be appreciated by making an alpine sink garden. This can be placed on a patio or near the house so that the plants' minute beauty can be seen easily. Bigger rockeries are often accompanied by water features (see Chapter 4); the earth dug out for a pond, for example, can be used to build up a rockery.

A properly crafted rockery can be a fascinating part of the garden, whether it has a mainly practical function of holding back a bank, for example, or merely as a feature in the corner of the garden or the lawn.

DESIGN

The best designer to learn from in this case, is mother nature herself. Those rock gardens that give the impression that they are 'growing' out of the ground with the main portion of rock still under the surface, like natural outcrops, look the most effective. If you take a trip to Wales or Scotland, you will see what I mean.

Rocks can be used to hold back an existing bank of soil, instead of a costly retaining brick wall. This can double-up as a natural-looking rock garden and combined with the mat-forming alpines will hold the soil back very efficiently.

If you're having the job done by a professional, always ask to see a previous job or photographs as not all gardeners can create an effective rockery.

SITING

Most alpine plants love the sun so try not to position the rockery in the shade. Shade caused by trees brings further problems in the autumn – fallen leaves left lying on alpines will quickly cause them to rot.

SMALL ROCK FEATURES

You don't need a lot of space to create a mini rock feature. I've built one very successfully on a large patio as a striking focal point, using large pieces of rock to build up the sides. Miniature conifers and shrubs and colourful alpine plants and bulbs were used to fill the top and planted in gaps in between the rocks. The addition of this simple feature enabled the client to grow plants that had proved difficult in the rest of her rather wet and shady garden.

WATER FEATURE

If you have children and you don't wish to have a pond, why not consider a recycling stream running through the rock garden? The pump sits in a tank at the base of the stream covered with pebbles. This circulates the water up to the top of the stream in a continuous cycle.

MATERIALS AND MECHANICS

THE ROCKS

Your local rock is probably cheaper than imported material, as delivery is very expensive. It will also look more natural in its home territory. Sandstone rock, if you can use this, looks very warm. It has straight edges and a squarish shape, ideal for an 'outcrop' design. Natural rocks should be hand-picked; this way, just the right pieces can be chosen.

You often see chunks of concrete or broken slabs used as rock substitutes which always look cheap and nasty. On the other hand, artificial, moulded rock made from concrete is much lighter and easier to work with than natural rock and can look very realistic. Trailing alpines cascading over them, and moss and lichens starting to take hold on the artificial surface will help to create a 'natural' look.

Hollow, man-made rocks are very useful if building a small feature on a roof garden, as weight is no longer a problem. I have also built beautiful rock schemes in bank foyers with cascading water, which would be impossible with the real thing.

Painting sour milk onto man-made rocks will encourage lichens and mosses.

If using squarish or angular rock, try to keep the natural grain horizontal. This will look far more natural.

Take care when handling rocks, as even seemingly small pieces can be very heavy. (Bend the knees, not the back!)

BUILDING THE ROCKERY

A tiered, or stepped design, is the most effective way of building a natural-looking rockery. This is particularly good for the plants, as the level areas behind the rocks allow the rain to soak in rather than running off a sheer slope (which is how they are often built). If the rocks are sloped back slightly, it not only looks authentic, but also guides the rain water back to the plants behind.

Always start building from the outer edge and work gradually inwards.

A rockery should always look natural, as if it was part of the landscape.

Try and create a V- or L-formation of rocks: one line set back from the other creates a 'step-up' effect. The first rock, or keystone, is usually the largest and forms the front or corner of the V. The rocks then get progressively smaller towards the back. The V-formation is not a rigid rule but it does make it easier to start off the rockery this way.

Bed rocks down firmly so they don't move when they're walked on. If laid cleverly, the rocks will allow you easy access around the area and make maintenance far easier.

Always use sterilized topsoil when building your rock garden, as perennial weeds amongst rock and alpine are very difficult to eradicate.

HYPERTUFA FOR ALPINES

Tufa rock is a lightweight, soft, porous limestone. By cutting out holes in the top and sides of the rock, alpines that require very free-draining conditions can be grown very easily. Lewisias grow particularly well like this. However, tufa is expensive and quite difficult to obtain. You can make your own out of hypertufa, an imitation rock which can be moulded to a desired shape and drilled like real tufa. Alternatively it can be moulded over boxes or old sinks:

- Stand the sink in the final position.
- Score the glazing off the sink first and apply a coat of epoxy glue to give a 'key' to the hypertufa mixture.
- Mix 1 part sand, 2 parts peat and 1 part cement.
- Add water until the mixture is like a stiff porridge.
- Plaster the mixture over the box or sink in a 2.5 cm (1 in) layer, with an 8 cm (3 in) layer over the lip inside.
- The coating, when set, can be chipped to give it a weathered appearance; alternatively, spread a little yogurt over it and eventually moss and lichen will develop.
- Fill with a layer of stones and compost. Plant up with alpines, a rock or two and a dwarf conifer for a 'genuine' look and add a layer of stone chippings to the surface.

PLANTINGS FOR ROCK GARDENS

ALPINES

Most garden centres and nurseries carry a large stock of rockery plants, which can give colour throughout the year. Most are hardy, generally easy to keep and very low-growing. For the more select or rare species you may need to seek out a specialist alpine grower. Many of the rare or unusual plants are uncommon for a reason, however: they're either very slow to propagate, or they're difficult to grow. If you're just starting off, you definitely need fool-proof plants!

In nature, many alpines are covered in snow throughout the winter. This insulative covering stops them getting much colder than freezing point; the soil is frozen, but dry! This is why alpines often rot off and die in our mild, wet winters.

Drainage therefore, is essential when planting alpines. As the rockery is raised, this will obviously help, but extra precautions, such as incorporating grit into the soil, are essential.

Points to remember include:

- Alpines spread quickly, so don't overplant.
- Don't feed alpines, as they are not hungry plants.
- Trim back alpines just after flowering, to encourage bushy growth.
- To fill a largish area of soil, plant alpines in groups of three of the same variety about 20 cm (8 in) apart for best effect.
- Water well, particularly in the first year, as any raised area will dry out quickly.

ACID-LOVING PLANTS

If you want to grow lime-hating plants and your garden soil is quite alkaline, then you could use your rock garden as a raised bed and use lime-free soil. This would enable you to grow the dwarf rhododendrons and azaleas with lime-hating alpines such as some gentians, and the delightful rhodohypoxis and lithospermum. (See the plant lists for further details.)

Some alpines such as aubrieta and arabis do not seem to mind where they go and are often used in ordinary borders as an edging plant, as are helianthemum (rock rose) and armeria (thrift).

Most are very easy to propagate by cuttings, or by seed, but the easiest way is to divide small rooted plantlets from the main plant, and grow them on in small pots, then plant them in their new position when established.

The foliage of some alpines is just as impressive as the flowering on others: try *Sedum acre* var. *aureum* (bright yellow), sagina (limey yellow), *Sedum spurium* 'Dragon's Blood' and other sedums (stonecrops in various shades).

A layer of grit on the soil around the alpines, will keep moisture in, deter slugs, look good and help prevent weed growth and mud splashing on flowers in heavy rain. In short, very beneficial!

Spring-flowering alpines

- *Anemone pulsatilla*. Huge, exotic-looking blooms in mid- to late spring; needs well-drained soil.
- *Alyssum saxatile*. Bright, golden yellow flowers in mid-spring to early summer; very tough; good contrast with aubrieta.
- Arabis. Colours range from white to purple-pink; evergreen foliage making good ground cover in sun; flowers late winter to early summer.
- Arenaria. Carpeting evergreen with tiny leaves and white flowers in early spring to mid-summer.
- Aubrieta. Very popular evergreen ground-cover plant; flowers, ranging from lilac to red, early spring to early summer.
- Erinus. Evergreen foliage; bright pink flowers over a long period from early spring to late summer.
- Myosotis (forget-me-not). Can be used as a short-term guest in large rockeries, but make sure it doesn't set seed everywhere, as it can be difficult to weed out; a bright splash of blue in spring–summer and cheap to buy in boxes in autumn–spring.
- *Primula* × *auricula*. Evergreen, leathery foliage; various colours from yellow to purple; flowers from early to mid-spring.
- *Primula rosea*. Narrow leaves and rose-pink, delicate flowers on 15 cm (6 in) stems in early to late spring.
- Raoulia. Almost like a silvery moss, but firm to the touch; very tight, low-spreading habit; tiny yellow flowers in late spring.
- Rhodohypoxis. Rose-red flowers from mid-spring to early autumn; needs well-drained acid soil.
- Saxifraga. Many species flower from early spring onwards, ranging from white to red; dense, succulent foliage, forming neat clumps that are fun to touch.

Early summer-flowering alpines

- Ajuga (bugle). Low, carpeting habit, sometimes invasive, with attractive foliage and blue-pink upright flowers in early summer; good in moist soil and can tolerate shade.
- Antennaria. Low, carpeting growth with tiny leaves; white or pink flowers in late spring to early summer.
- Aquilegia (columbine). Rockery types available in blue to white; sun or partial shade; flowers early to mid-summer.
- Dianthus (alpine pink). Many species flower from late spring onwards, forming dense mounds of silvery foliage and beautiful pink-red flowers; limey soil in sun is best.
- Erysimum (alpine wallflower). Not too long-lived, but still well worth growing; bright yellow flowers in late spring to early summer; limey soil in sun.
- *Gentiana acaulis*. Huge, deep blue, bell-like flowers in late spring to early summer. Best in neutral-acid, moisture-retentive, but well-drained soil.
- *Geranium cinereum*. Low, spreading version of its more robust relatives; dazzling dark cerise-purple flowers in late spring to mid-autumn.
- Iberis. Brilliant, white flowers smothering the plant in late spring to mid-summer; a definite must!
- Lewisia. A choice plant that needs a bit of loving care; plant between cracks at an angle in the rocks so that the rain doesn't sit in its crown and rot it; superb, exotic-looking flowers from late spring to mid-summer.

- Lithospermum. Dazzling blue flowers over long period; evergreen foliage, shrubby habit; needs neutral to acid soil.
- Lychnis (campion). Tufted habit, with deep rose-pink flowers from late spring to mid-summer; sunny well-drained spot.
- Oxalis. Tiny, silvery leaved, clump-forming alpine; grows from a corm; needs well-drained soil; beautiful pink flowers in late spring to mid-summer; *O. adenophylla* will be too invasive for rockeries.
- Phlox. Most alpine phlox are in flower from late spring onwards; low, neat, carpeting habit; superb cascading over rocks and walls; flowers pink, lavender or white.
- Silene. Vigorous creeper, with vivid pink flowers in late spring to early summer.
- Thymus (thyme). Low, creeping plant with aromatic foliage and masses of lilac, pink or white flowers from late spring.
- Veronica. Carpeting alpine with pink, red or blue flowers from late spring; quite vigorous, so keep a check on it.
- Viola. Different species flower for most of the summer; boxes of plants are good value as 'fillers' on a new or large rockery.

Mid- to late summer-flowering alpines

- *Aster alpinus*. Tough little customer that spreads quickly and bears purple-lilac flowers in mid- to late summer; mildew not normally a problem.
- *Astilbe chinensis*. Miniature cousin of the poolside astilbe; rose-purple flowers from mid-summer to mid-autumn; best in moist soil, sun or semi-shade.

A sink garden is the perfect environment for alpines that require good drainage.

- Campanula. There are many excellent campanula; all are tough and easy to grow; variations of white, blue or purple bell-like flowers from early summer.
- Gentiana. Some of these choice plants flower from mid- to late summer (*G. septemfida*), or early to late autumn (*G. sinoornata*); best in peaty soil that stays moist, but not waterlogged.
- *Geranium cinereum* 'Ballerina'. Deep pink flowers from early summer to autumn; neat clump-forming perennial, but not for the tiny rock garden.
- *Geranium dalmaticum*. Light pink, delicate flowers from early to late summer; small, segmented leaves and low, spreading habit.

- Gypsophila. The alpine version is a worthy addition to the rockery, or raised bed; white or pink flower sprays from early summer, sometimes into mid-autumn (*G. cerastioides*).
- Helianthemum (rock rose). Evergreen plant with attractive leaves all year, smothered in poppy-like flowers in early to late summer in white, red, pink or yellow.
- Hypericum. There are some beautiful, tiny alpine species not to be confused with the invasive and impossible to eradicate *H. calycinum*; small bright yellow flowers mid-summer to early autumn.
- Leontopodium (edelweis). Silvery leaves with white-grey unusual flowers appearing from early to mid-summer; needs very good drainage; flowers pure white in their natural mountain habitat.
- Lithospermum (see page 25).
- Saponaria (tumbling Ted). One of my favourites for a large rockery as it does grow quickly; absolutely covered in shocking pink flowers in its main flowering period from early to mid-summer; great to cascade over rocks or raised bed.
- Sempervivum (houseleek). Interesting, succulent, pointed leaves; can tolerate hardly any moisture and minimum soil; good between rocks or roof tiles; long stems with superb pink-red flowers in summer.
- Thymus (thyme). Some flower late such as *T. serpyllum*; mat-forming, aromatic foliage with pink or white flowers in mid- to late summer.

Natural rock and rockery plants are often successfully used to retain banks and raised beds.

DWARF EVERGREEN SHRUBS

- Andromeda. Tiny-leaved shrub that needs a lime-free soil; delicate pink or white bell-like flowers in spring.
- *Berberis* × *stenophylla* 'Irwinii'. Tough, prickly foliage and hanging clusters of bright yellow flowers in spring and early summer.
- *Buxus sempervirens* 'Suffruticosa' (box). This is the tiniest form which can be clipped to any shape or size.
- Cistus (see page 14 and 73).
- Euonymus. Very hardy with variegated leaves; clip to keep in check.
- Genista. There are some tiny ones, but for a large rockery, *G. lydia* is excellent but it spreads quite wide; arching stems smothered in yellow flowers late spring to early summer.
- Hebe. Most of the small-leaved varieties are ideal; flowers ranging from white to blue in summer; *H.* 'Mrs Winder' has purple leaves (see also page 74 and 79).
- Lavandula (lavender). Dwarf varieties are perfect; aromatic foliage, bright blue flowers in mid-summer. (See also page 74.)
- Penstemon (see page 15 and 72).
- Rhododendron. There are many miniature rhododendron varieties available for the rock garden; add plenty of peat or composted bark to soil.

DWARF DECIDUOUS SHRUBS

- *Berberis thunbergii* 'Atropurpurea Nana'. Deep wine-red leaves that turn rich fiery-orange in autumn; tight, bushy habit.

- Ceratostigma. Bright blue flowers in late summer; good for largish rock garden.
- Caryopteris. Bright blue flowers in late summer; cut back hard in spring; good for largish rockery.
- *Daphne* × *burkwoodii* 'Somerset'. Can keep some leaves through winter; upright bushy habit; richly scented reddish-pink flowers in late spring to early summer; for the larger rock garden.
- Perovskia. Another late-flowering blue, with aromatic foliage; cut back after flowering; only for the larger rock garden.
- *Potentilla fruticosa*. Some of the dwarf varieties are ideal; 'Pretty Polly' is a newish pink one and 'Tilford Cream' is another smaller variety ideal for the rock garden.
- Roses. Miniature roses give tremendous value as they flower for most of the summer; must be watered regularly; cut back to a stump in spring; 'County' roses are also ideal, but they may spread too much for a small rockery (see page 74).
- *Spiraea japonica* 'Little Princess'. Fluffy pink flowers in mid-summer.

DWARF CONIFERS

Many conifers claim to be dwarf, but after 10 years, may be as much as 1.2 m (4 ft) high, or more. This is no good for the average rock feature, unless you want to trim them twice a year, which will restrict their growth, so check carefully before buying.

Conifers are often the 'backbone' to the rock garden, with their striking foliage, often changing colour with the seasons. Never overplant with conifers or you will lose their individual beauty. Treat them as spot accent plants.

Spray conifers, especially 'needled' species, against red spider and aphids throughout the summer. 'Rapid' is not harmful to bees, ladybirds or hover-flies, which are beneficial to the garden.

Here are a few true dwarfs:

- *Chamaecyparis lawsoniana* 'Ellwoods Pillar' is very dense with upright habit, dark green. *C.l.* 'Ellwoods Gold' has lovely golden foliage, dense and upright, but will probably be 1 m (3 ft) in 10 years, unless in poor, dry soil. *C.l.* 'Minima Aurea' is my favourite dwarf conifer with soft limey-yellow foliage and neat habit. *C.l.* 'Minima Glauca' has rounded habit and neat vertical sprays of foliage.
- *Chamaecyparis obtusa* 'Nana Lutea'. Yellow, curly foliage; very slow-growing.
- *Chamaecyparis pisifera*. 'Filifera Nana' has mop-like, shaggy habit, low but quite wide-spreading.
- *Chamaecyparis thyoïdes* 'Red Star' is green in summer, plum purple in winter and very slow-growing.
- *Juniperus communis* 'Compressa'. Miniature alpine conifer, ideal for sink gardens; dense, upright habit; blue-grey foliage.
- *Juniperus squamata* 'Blue Star'. Steely blue foliage; tight, bushy habit; very slow.
- *Picea glauca* var. *albertiana* 'Conica'. Tight conical habit; new growth is lush lime-green; spray from early spring.
- *Picea pungens* 'Globosa'. Dwarf blue spruce that only grows 2–5 cm (1–2 in) per year; spray from early spring.

- *Pinus mugo* 'Mops'. Tiny pine ideal for rock garden; works well as bonsai specimen.
- *Thuja occidentalis* 'Danica'. Rich green foliage; dense rounded habit; very slow.
- *Thuja orientalis* 'Aurea Nana'. Beautiful variety with golden upright sprays of foliage and a neat, oval habit.
- *Thuja plicata* 'Rogersii'. True dwarf; dense, upright habit, with yellow flecked foliage.

HEATHERS

Most heathers do not like lime at their roots, nor a heavy, or wet soil. They grow far more happily in full sun, in a light, peaty-type soil which doesn't get too dry, nor too wet in winter. *Erica carnea* (winter-flowering heather), however, can be grown almost anywhere except deep shade.

I always plant heathers in groups of three or more of the same variety, about 30 cm (12 in) apart; this gives a much stronger effect. Plant in autumn to spring as they may dry out too quickly in summer.

DWARF BULBS

There are numerous miniature bulbs that fit perfectly into the rock scene. They look effective in clumps of one variety.

Miniature tulips love well-drained sunny sites and tiny narcissus look wonderful amongst alpines and dwarf conifers. Other favourites are crocus, colchicum and galanthus (snowdrop). (See also page 45.)

The Rock Garden

Avner and Rebecca had all the makings of a superb rock garden in their suburban back yard, but unfortunately it was completely covered in rampant weeds and overgrown perennials! There was a mound of earth and a few pieces of concrete could be glimpsed through the undergrowth. A crumbled concrete waterfall led down to what looked like the rim of a concrete pond. A now huge conifer was the only surviving worthwhile plant on the whole rock garden. It was probably 60 years old highlighting the fact that even very slow-growing conifers can eventually grow very large. A fairly large *Prunus cerasifera* 'Nigra' (purple-leaved plum) balanced the conifer and was a beautiful tree not casting too much shade onto the area.

Believe it or not, this was once a rockery.

Give new plants plenty of room to grow.

OPPOSITE *The natural tiered effect of the new rockery will soon be disguised by the plants.*

Materials

2 tons of Purbeck rockery stone
2 tons of sterilized topsoil
6 × 25 kg (55 lb) bags of washed grit
Butyl liner
3 × 1.8 × 1.8 m (6 × 6 ft) trellis panels
4 × 2.5 m (8 ft) posts
Windbreak netting

Design

We decided to keep the conifer and the prunus. The top of the *Chamaecyparis obtusa* had a different foliage to the bottom as it was reverting back to its wild origins, which often happens with mature specimens. This could be pruned.

We decided on using a sandstone rock, which was just right for the tiered design of rock garden I wanted to achieve.

The old waterfall was pretty much central to the scheme, so we decided to create a sort of 'grotto', or mini-cave.

Step-by-step

1 The clearance and pruning All the weeds and overgrown perennials were removed and the concrete lumps taken away. The rogue limb of the conifer was removed which actually balanced up the whole shape. The old pond, which had been filled in, was excavated to reveal a solid concrete shell.

2 The rocks and soil We selected about 2 tons of rock, which I hand-picked to get just the right shapes and sizes.

The V-formation design was used (see page 22) and once the first line was in place, the area behind was filled with sterilized topsoil and firmed down, to the height of the top of the rock. The second line started approx 60 cm (2 ft) back from the first, leaving plenty of room for plants. This process continued until the rocks were being laid on the old rockery site and around the conifer.

Where the waterfall was, our 'grotto' was formed by using some flat, wide rocks and laying them across the 'ravine' resting on stable rocks each side.

3 The plants To give the large conifer some company, we planted a selection of dwarf conifers that had different shape and colour interests. These would be the 'backbone' of the rockery, giving height and definition, even in winter. These would be trimmed each summer to keep them in check.

Some small, flowering shrubs were used staggered between the conifers to give colour, none of which would grow too tall.

The icing on the cake is always the plants. I used most in groups of three and other single specimens in the gaps in between the rocks.

Fine, washed grit was used while planting to help drainage. It was also spread around the plants afterwards.

4 The pool Unfortunately, the old pond was slightly cracked, but by lining it with a Butyl liner and filling it with water, the pond was quickly renovated. We used flattish rocks to hide the edges, and a few bunches of oxygenating weed to keep the water fresh and encourage wildlife (see Chapter 4).

5 The background screen To define the rock garden and screen off the vegetable area at the end of the garden, we used trellis panels with plastic windbreak netting. This really made the rock garden stand out and hid the area behind, allowing light and wind to be filtered through the netting.

PLANTS USED FOR THE TV GARDEN

Conifers

- 1 × *Thuja occidentalis* 'Holmstrup'. Deep green, soft foliage; neat, conical habit; slow growth; 90 × 30 cm (3 × 1 ft) in 10 years.
- 1 × *Thuja occidentalis* 'Golden Globe'. Soft, golden foliage; rounded habit; 90 × 90 cm (3 × 3 ft) in 10 years.
- 1 × *Thuja occidentalis* 'Danica'. Deep green foliage; very slow-growing; rounded habit; 60 × 60 cm (24 × 24 in) in 10 years.
- 1 × *Chamaecyparis pisifera* 'Filifera Variegata'. Mop-like habit; yellow-flecked foliage; 75 × 90 cm (30 in × 3 ft) in 10 years.
- 1 × *Chamaecyparis pisifera* 'Nana'. Very slow, tight habit; deep green foliage; 45 × 60 cm (17 × 24 in) in 10 years.
- 1 × *Chamaecyparis lawsoniana* 'Ericoides'. Limey-green in summer, changing to plum-purple in winter; soft, feathery foliage; bushy habit; 90 × 90 cm (3 × 3 ft) in 10 years.

Dwarf shrubs

- 1 × *Potentilla fruticosa* 'Pretty Polly'
- 1 × *Cistus* 'Decumbens'
- 1 × *Convolvulus cneorum*. Silver-leaved small shrub with large white flowers in summer; likes well-drained position in full sun; 40 × 50 cm (16 × 20 in).
- 12 × various heathers
- 1 × *Spiraea japonica* 'Little Princess'

Alpines

- 12 × aubrieta
- 6 × arabis
- 6 × alyssum
- 3 × campanula
- 3 × carex (sedge). Evergreen grass with golden striped leaves; likes sun or semi-shade; 23 × 30 cm (9 × 12 in).
- 6 × erodium. Tiny relative of perennial geranium; dainty pink flowers over a long period from mid-summer; likes sunny position in well-drained soil.
- 3 × gypsophila
- 3 × *Geranium sanguineum*. Magenta pink flowers and deeply divided leaves; low-spreading growth; 30 × 45 cm (12 × 18 in).
- 6 × helianthemum
- 3 × iberis
- 3 × primula
- 6 × saxifrage
- 6 × sedum

chapter three

The Shady Garden

If you happen to live in Spain or another hot, sunny climate where light levels are high, a shady garden would be a definite advantage, as tree shade can protect plants. Here in the UK, trees can create a rather gloomy picture, with plants struggling to get enough light and a deluge of fallen leaves occurring in winter. Shade can be created by buildings or by your own house if the garden is facing north. Another problem can be caused by competition from tree roots if there are too many trees dominating. Trees will deprive other plants of moisture, nutrient levels and light.

However, the notion that a shady garden is a real problem is largely unjustified. Obviously there are certain plant species that do not grow well in these conditions, but paradoxically many other plants thrive here. (See the planting section, page 40).

A shady site should not be a problem area as many plants such as ferns grow happily without much sun. Ensure wooden decking is kept algae-free and use annuals in tubs to add a splash of colour.

DESIGN

Design is very important in this type of garden and careful thought must be paid to plant choice, not merely for flower colour, but for foliage, texture, habit and form. Using focal points such as statuary or ornaments, you can create a beautiful garden of lush foliage and strong features. Who needs lavender and roses!

DESIGNS TO AVOID

Certain styles of garden are definitely out. The traditional rose garden, for instance, is a waste of time: low light levels will mean weak growth and poor flower quality. Lawn areas also suffer in shade, with mossy patches becoming a problem.

Never position a greenhouse in shade, as seedlings generally need good light for strong growth. Most vegetables need sun to crop well.

Building a rockery is not advisable in shade, as most alpines need sun and dryish conditions.

They may survive, but will not flourish and flower well.

Heather gardens will certainly be a waste of money. Leggy, poor-flowering plants will result.

POSSIBILITIES

A standard water garden scheme is normally a no-go area, especially if you wish to grow water lilies, marginal plants and keep fish: high-tech filtration and aeration systems will be needed to keep the water clean and healthy, and special lighting to enhance the colours of the fish. Leaves and debris build up in a pond to render it lifeless.

Water can be introduced, however, in other ways. The sound of running water can be achieved without the need for a still pool: a recycling stream, for instance, will create a wonderful effect without the maintenance problems associated with the more conventional pond feature. Gurgling water amongst rounded cobbles, or trickling over a millstone, works really well to give the sight and sound effect without the need for fish and water plants.

Wall-mounted water features are perfect for a shady garden and can be a strong focal point on a wall or fence. They are usually made of moulded concrete or terracotta, although there are some good plastic imitations also available which are much cheaper. Most of them contain a small well-disguised pump.

A simple water-filled half-barrel makes an effective water feature especially if used with a pump to make a small fountain. In shade, algal growth is not such a problem, but obviously falling leaves will have to be removed in autumn.

Filling the barrel or container with cobbles will further cut down the maintenance and will also render the feature far safer if young children are present.

Woodland scenes are wonderfully relaxing and can be imitated here. Plants such as bamboo, ferns, hostas and rhododendrons, all grow well and with the inclusion of mossy boulders, an oriental atmosphere can easily be achieved.

Here are a few points to consider when designing a shady garden:

● Low light intensity means careful planning will be needed when working out the planting scheme. Subtle pruning of overgrown, overhanging trees will let more light in. Competition from invading roots can be avoided by root pruning which is best undertaken in winter. Positioning paving stones vertically in the ground may hold back the invasion for a few years. Otherwise, introduce at least 30 cm (12 in) of fresh topsoil above the root level, keeping it off the trunk; this will help to establish new plants.
● If you need a lawn area, certain grass species are better suited to shade and special grass seed is available at most garden centres.
● Algae and moss grow happily in shady conditions: keep paths and walkways clean and free from growth with the use of moss killer to prevent them becoming too slippery in winter – a safety point to look out for especially with old people and children.
● Artificial lighting is an excellent way to introduce light into an otherwise gloomy garden or dark corners. Lights can be cleverly hidden amongst plants to add to the effect. A

skilled electrician should always be called in to tackle any electrical work in the garden. Lighting can extend your pleasure of the garden through the long winter evenings. Deciduous shrubs and trees can take on beautiful shapes when lit in a certain way. Silver birch look wonderful lit from below, upwards into the winter night.

● Using light-coloured paving and painting wood and brickwork white can really brighten up a shady area. If natural timber is required, use a clear preservative or use tanalized wood which is light green.

● Never use gravel under trees, as it soon becomes clogged with leaves and is therefore very difficult to keep clean.

STYLES AND THEMES

There are two obvious styles for this type of garden, informal and formal. The use of plants may be similar in both, but the whole structure of the garden is totally different.

I have seen shady gardens that have taken ideas from both styles, which can work very well.

INFORMAL SHADY GARDEN

Most people, I find, prefer a natural-looking scheme, something to bring them back to nature.

Hard landscaping

Hard landscaping first is very important for access and patios. Position these in the design early.

For the informal design, curved lines for paths work best; take care not to make them too curvy, or short cuts will be taken.

To get the flow right, always walk around the garden to see where the natural walkways are. Then mark them out with a hosepipe and stand back to see how they work visually. Remember, that once low perennials or shrubs have grown round the edges, the curve will look much less severe.

Paving stones in shade can become very slippery with algae, so non-slip paving is best.

Wooden decking looks wonderful with lush foliage plants, but it must be kept free of algae.

Light-coloured paving will certainly help to brighten up dark areas in the garden. If pale paving looks a bit out of place with a dark red brick house, for example, why not edge it with red frost-proof bricks which would not only hold the patio together visually, but would also link it with the building.

Mirrors work brilliantly, not only to increase the image of space, but the reflection also improves the feeling of light, especially if positioned cleverly. I always like to frame the mirror with an archway of some sort, be it wood or metal. I have also seen a wrought-iron gate image painted on a curved-top mirror and fixed to a wall. The effect was very impressive. A whole new garden with no extra maintenance!

Soft landscaping

If left to its own devices, a plot of land in shade will soon be colonized by native and introduced plant species: plants such as foxgloves, bluebells and wild anemones, may appear on their own accord.

Unfortunately, we are all too impatient to wait for this natural cycle, and would probably prefer some of the more traditional garden plants.

If the totally natural look is what you are seeking, then simply take a hike to your local woodland to see what nature has created for itself. Remember not to take native plants from the wild as they rarely grow once transplanted, and many are now scarce in their native habitat.

Wild plant seeds are available at garden centres and even young plants are easily purchased. Foxgloves, forget-me-nots, *Anemone nemerosa*, primroses and oxlips all grow happily in semi-shade.

Planting in swathes and groups creates a natural feel, I often favour bold groups of one type of plant, say hosta or astilbe. This gives a stronger impact, rather than too much of a mixture, which can look 'bitty'.

FORMAL SHADY GARDEN

The great formal gardens of the world are noted for their symmetrical lines, rows of clipped hedges with topiary and grand statues and water fountains.

Formal gardens are making a bit of a comeback, especially in suburban areas, where symmetry and strong lines are in keeping with the modern house and surroundings.

The grand style can be mimicked to fit into a shady garden, by using the same design principles, but obviously the choice of plants will have to be carefully considered. Formal gardens are normally in full sun.

The benefit of opting for a formal style is that plants almost play second-fiddle to focal points and features. This can be very useful, especially if the shade cast on your garden is so severe that very few plants can really grow successfully.

Focal points

Tasteful statues and self-circulating fountains can look magnificent at the end of a path or against a dull wall.

The effect I try to achieve is one where only a single focal point is visible from any position in the garden. This can be done by simply using evergreen plants, or even trellis work, to disguise the statue or feature from unwanted angles.

The lighter the colour, the more striking the effect will be, but old mossy statues or urns may look more subtle and mysterious.

Paths and borders

Paths need not run straight from the house. Diagonal lines work really well and everything, including the beds, will then run at an angle of 45 degrees. This design is especially useful if you wish to take the eye away from the back wall, for instance, or guide the eye to a natural focal point.

If you start the diagonal theme from the house, by laying paving at 45 degrees from it, note that you will have to cut many slabs. This can be avoided by simply filling in the gaps between house and paving with ornamental gravel.

Hedging and topiary

Yew and box plants will tolerate some shade, but will not thrive in very dark conditions. Also note that yew is poisonous (except the red flesh of the fruits). Yew is used for hedges of 1 m (3 ft) and over, box for hedges from 30 cm (12 in) high and over. Clipped box in large pots or urns in interesting topiary designs never fail to impress. Even without the addition of colourful flowers, they have a timeless beauty that never goes out of fashion. Start off with a young plant and clip to shape over four to five years. Pinch new shoots back in summer.

The symmetry of low, geometric hedges adds to the formality of the scheme and when combined with focal points and seasonal colour, a dazzling impression can be made.

Other plants that are ideal for low hedges will be covered in the planting section (page 118).

Shady areas can be transformed into very romantic gardens.

HOW TO TAKE BOX CUTTINGS

Box (*Buxus*) cuttings are best taken from mid-summer to autumn. Short lengths are cut off about 5–6 cm (2–2¾ in) down from the tip. Remove the lower leaves about 2 cm (¾ in) up from the cut, and ensure the cut is clean and preferably just below a leaf joint. Dip the end in rooting compound or liquid and insert in half peat, half sharp sand mix. Water thoroughly, then cover with a plastic bag or place in a shady cold frame. Bottom heat with heating cables will speed up their rooting. I always pack the cuttings quite close together in a seed tray or pot and spray them with water every one or two days to prevent the foliage drying out.

Rooting should take about six to eight weeks after which time they can be potted up individually in 6 cm (2 in) pots and grown on until the following autumn. They can then be planted out or potted on.

PLANTINGS FOR SHADY GARDENS

As I have mentioned earlier, choosing plants need not be as daunting a prospect as you might imagine. There really is a huge choice if you go to a good nursery, at the right time of year.

Spring and early summer are good times to buy any plants, as nowadays young specimens in small pots are readily available at this time. After this they can become pot-bound and the choice is more limited. Small plants will soon catch up on the larger sizes and are usually half the price!

YEAR-ROUND INTEREST

Many shade-tolerant plants and bulbs flower only in the spring and early summer. This is because in nature this is the only time of year that sufficient light is available before the trees come into leaf. So all the reproduction is carried out at this time.

This is fine in nature, but in the garden setting, it can mean a flurry of interest in spring and no further flower colour for the rest of the year. Some plants such as hellebores, snowdrops and aconites flower as early as December, making use of the brighter environment. Careful planning must be made to ensure year-round interest.

Don't be unduly worried about lack of colour, as there are a surprising amount of plant species that enjoy and thrive in this type of environment. Many of these can be very colourful indeed. Avoid bright red, vivid orange and most blue flowers (except myosotis, brunnera and omphalodes) which are usually associated with sunnier gardens.

The best thing to do if you want colour in summer, is to use bedding plants. Busy Lizzies and begonias are the two main annual species that will grow happily in low light levels.

FOLIAGE EFFECTS

Evergreen, glossy-leaved shrubs are well suited to shady areas, as the shiny surface of the leaves reflect off each other, maximizing every ray of light. This is why ivy, laurel and holly are all found in woodlands. Also the leathery, glossy foliage helps to prevent the build-up of honeydew falling from surrounding trees.

Specimen plants and shrubs with strong shapes and varying leaf shades and textures should be the main backbone of your garden. Beautiful gardens do not necessarily need a mass of bright colours.

GROUP PLANTING

I generally plant perennials in groups of three or more. This gives a bold effect and the plants look much happier this way. Group plantings of one flower colour are also very effective, but having said that, a mixture of astilbe blooms, for instance, can look superb.

The striking foliage of hostas look particularly strong in clumps of one variety.

For a natural look, vary the heights and textures of the groups, with the addition of the odd taller shrub to give a lift.

TIPS ON PLANTING

● To create an informal winding effect out of a straight path, plant groups of alchemilla on each side. Do not plant the groups opposite each other.
● Soft fruit and fruit trees really prefer sun to grow and prosper. However, the Morello cherry does actually flower and fruit well on a north-facing wall, so there's one to try.
● When planting a tall-growing bamboo, remember that they often spread quite quickly by suckering. By planting them in a bottomless tub, the bamboo can be contained by restricting sideways expansion.

● If you really want a rock garden, why not keep it very simple and grow *Vinca minor* (periwinkle), mind-your-own-business, London pride and maybe dwarf ferns and mosses. The effect will be very different to a normal rockery, but still interesting.
● Conifers really prefer sun, but there are a few thujas and yews that will tolerate some shade.

SHRUBS

● *Acer palmatum* 'Atropurpureum' (purple Japanese maple). The usual *Acer palmatum* has soft green leaves and is larger than this variety; both are deciduous; all Japanese maples are ideal for light shade, but this one is my first choice; it introduces a purple foliage giving a striking contrast to a green garden and colouring up beautifully in autumn; acers also do very well in containers; 1.5–1.8 m (5–6 ft) × 90 cm–1.2 m (3–4 ft) in 10 years.
● *Acer japonicum* 'Aconitifolium' (Japanese maple). Deciduous; large, dissected light green leaves, colouring up beautifully in autumn to orange-red; mound-forming; 90 cm–1.2 m (3–4 ft) × 90 cm–1.2 m (3–4 ft) in 10 years.
● *Aucuba japonica* 'Variegata' (spotted laurel). Evergreen; common, but a very worthwhile plant; lush, shiny leaves always looking attractive and on 'female' plants bright red berries are often seen for many months of the year; *A.j.* 'Rozannie' is a relatively new Dutch hybrid with dark green leaves and larger, more outstanding berries; 1.5–1.8 m (5–6 ft) × 90 cm–1.2 m (3–4 ft) in 10 years.

● Azaleas. All azaleas are really rhododendrons: *Rhododendron japonicum* (Japanese azalea) are evergreen, slow-growing shrubs which look attractive all year round, with masses of flowers in spring; various colours; needs slightly acid soil to do well; 60–90 cm (2–3 ft) in 10 years. The Mollis azaleas are deciduous, taller and more upright than the Japanese azalea; leaves turn rich orange-red in autumn; many have scented flowers in early summer; needs slightly acid soil; 1.2–1.5 m (4–5 ft) × 60–90 cm (2–3 ft) in 10 years.

● *Buxus* (box). Evergreen, slow-growing and ideal for clipping; grows equally well in a container, but remember this will need more watering; *B. sempervirens* is used for topiary and taller hedges (see also page 38 and 39).

● Camellia. Dark green, evergreen leaves always looking lush and healthy even in winter; huge flowers in late winter to early spring; needs fairly acid soil; 1.2–1.5 m (4–5 ft) × 90 cm–1.2 m (3–4 ft) in 10 years.

● *Cornus alba* 'Spaethii' (golden dogwood). Deciduous; the golden foliage really cheers up a dull area, looking fresh and colourful all summer; dark red stems give winter interest; for the best stem colour use the green-leaved *C.a.* 'Sibirica', or for silvery variegation choose *C.a.* 'Elegantissima'; dogwoods prefer moist soil; prune hard each spring to produce the best stem colour; 1.5–2.1 m (5–7 ft) × 1.2–1.5 m (4–5 ft) in 10 years.

● *Cotoneaster* 'Cornubia'. Evergreen except in severe cold; white flowers followed by red berries; good for birds; vigorous growth; 1.8–2.1 m (6–7 ft) × 1.5–1.8 m (5–6 ft) in 10 years.

● *Eleagnus pungens* 'Maculata'. Evergreen; unbeatable golden variegated foliage that stays bright and cheerful through the winter; fairly slow growing but well worth the wait; best in light shade, as it will try to revert back to green in darker conditions; any green shoots should be pruned out quickly; 1.5–1.8 m (5–6 ft) × 1.5–1.8 m (5–6 ft) in 10 years.

● *Fatsia japonica* (castor oil plant). Evergreen; bold, architectural shiny leaves making a good specimen plant; white flowers in autumn; 1.2–1.5 m (4–5 ft) × 1.2–1.5 m (4–5 ft) in 10 years.

● *Hydrangea paniculata* 'Grandiflora'. Deciduous; a perfect choice where shade is not too dense; huge panicles of creamy white flowers in mid–late summer, which can look magnificent even in winter when covered in frost; prune all stems down to 60 cm (2 ft) in early spring; 1.5–2.1 m (5–7 ft) × 1.2–1.5 m (4–5 ft) in 10 years.

● *Hypericum* 'Hidcote'. Deciduous; very easy to grow with bright yellow flowers smothering the bush in mid–late summer; often looks better planted in a group of three, 60 cm–1 m (2–3 ft) apart; prune half-way back in spring; 1.2–1.5 m (4–5 ft) × 1.2–1.5 m (4–5 ft) in 10 years.

● *Ilex aquifolium* 'Pyramidalis' (thornless holly). Evergreen; a 'friendly' holly, with dark green, soft prickle-less leaves and offering a beautiful display of berries in late summer through winter; self-pollinating so does not need a 'male' plant to produce its crop of fruits; responds well to clipping and ideal for the formal setting; 1.8–2.1 m (6–7 ft) × 90 cm–1.2 m (3–4 ft) in 10 years.

● *Magnolia wilsonii*. Deciduous; pure white, cup-like flowers with red-purple stamens; later flowering than others and so less likely to be damaged by frost; 1.8–2.1 m (6–7 ft) × 1.2–1.5 m (4–5 ft) in 10 years.

● *Mahonia japonica*. Evergreen; striking, spiky foliage with large sprays of scented yellow flowers in winter/spring; good specimen plant; 1.8 × 1.2 m (6 × 4 ft) in 10 years.

● *Pieris* 'Forest Flame'. Evergreen; has many merits and grows well in shade; throughout

autumn/winter bears hanging creamy flower buds which open in spring to pure white, similar to lily-of-the-valley; while in flower, new bright red, beautiful growth appears; requires slightly acid soil; 90 cm–1.2 m (3–4 ft) × 90 cm–1.2 m (3–4 ft) in 10 years.

● *Rhododendron* hybrid 'Christmas Cheer'. Evergreen; one of the earliest rhododendrons to flower; pale pink trusses of flowers appear in early spring; low, spreading habit makes it ideal for tubs; slightly acid soil preferred; 90 cm–1.2 m (3–4 ft) × 1.2–1.5 m (4–5 ft) in 10 years. Most other hybrids are suitable for shade.

Water features can create sound and provide an impressive focal point.

GROUND-COVER SHRUBS

● *Cotoneaster dammeri*. Evergreen; very neat, flat habit; white flowers; red berries in autumn through winter; grows in most soils; 4 × 90 cm (2 in × 3 ft) in 5 years.

● *Euonymus fortunei* 'Emerald 'n' Gold'. Evergreen; excellent good-looking low cover in shade with variegated leaves; best planted in groups of three or more, 60 cm (2 ft) apart; variety 'Emerald Gaiety' has similar habit but silvery variegation; 45 × 60 cm (18 × 24 in) in 5 years.

● *Lonicera pileata*. Evergreen; very tough plant that quickly covers the ground; small leaves, neat growth; best planted in groups 45–60 cm (1½–2 ft) apart in sun or shade; 45 × 75 cm (18 × 30 in) in 5 years.

● *Prunus laurocerasus* 'Otto Luyken'. Evergreen; low-growing laurel ideal as ground cover under trees; dark green, shiny leaves are a superb background to the white candle-like flowers that sit vertically up the stems in early summer; best planted in groups; 45–60 cm (18 in–2 ft) × 75–90 cm (30 in–3 ft) in 5 years.

● *Viburnum davidii*. Evergreen; excellent ground cover with white flower heads and occasional blue fruits in autumn; 45 × 60 cm (18 × 24 in) in 5 years.

● *Vinca* (periwinkle). Evergreen; rather invasive plant with bright blue flowers in spring and periodically throughout the summer; good for mass planting schemes under trees; plant 30–40 cm (12–16 in) apart; *Vinca minor*: 15 × 75 cm (6 × 30 in) in 5 years; *Vinca major*: 45 × 90 cm (18 in × 3 ft) in 5 years.

CLIMBERS

● Chaenomeles (quince). Very showy crimson, white, pink or orange flowers in early spring on bare twigs; fruits may follow on single-petalled varieties; needs support.

● *Clematis montana*. Vigorous; flowers mid- to late spring; deep pink, pale pink or white forms available; *C. m.* 'Elizabeth' is my favourite; not good in very deep shade.

● × *Fatshedera lizei*. A cross between the castor oil plant (*Fatsia japonica*) and an ivy. The shade tolerance of both parents is manifested in this bold tolerant evergreen wall shrub; needs training; white flowers on older plants.

● Hedera (ivy). All are ideal for a shady site; all-green varieties are better suited for a very dark situation. *Hedera canariensis* 'Gloire de Marengo' is probably the most vigorous variegated form.

● *Hydrangea petiolaris* (climbing hydrangea). Quite slow to get going but well worth it; self-clinging deciduous plant with large creamy white flowerheads in mid- to late summer; 1.2 m × 90 cm (4 × 3 ft) in 3 years.

● Parthenocissus (Virginia creeper). Vigorous deciduous climber which turns rich red in autumn; grows anywhere and *P. tricuspidata* 'Veitchii' is self-clinging; 2.1 × 1.8 m (7 × 6 ft) in 3 years.

● Pyracantha (firethorn). Thorny evergreen shrub that needs support; glossy, dark green leaves and orange, red or yellow berries over a long period; covered in white flowers in early summer; not good in deep shade as this discourages the berrying; clip in summer to keep it close against the wall.

ANNUAL AND PERENNIAL PLANTS

See also perennials (page 70 and 72–3) in The Low-maintenance Garden chapter.

● Annuals such as impatiens (busy Lizzie) and begonias are superb plants for long-lasting colour throughout the summer.

● *Alchemila mollis* (lady's mantle). Useful tough plant with pale green leaves and feathery sprays of pale greeny-yellow flowers in summer; 45 × 60 cm (18 × 24 in).

● *Ajuga reptans* (bugle). Mat-forming stems with coloured foliage; dark purple or variegated; best in moist soil; 4 × 45 cm (2 × 18 in).

● *Anemone japonica*. Pink or white flowers held on high stems in late summer; 1.2 m × 60 cm (4 × 2 ft).

● Astilbe. Beautiful sprays of flowers in summer, from white to red; best in moist soil and light shade; about 60 × 60 cm (2 × 2 ft) (variable).

● *Bergenia cordata*. Leathery, evergreen leaves and pink, white or red flowers in spring; good ground cover; about 30 × 45 cm (12 × 18 in).

● Brunnera. Large, heart-shaped leaves with forget-me-not flowers in spring to early summer; good ground cover; 45 × 60 cm (18 × 24 in).

● Epimedium. Compact, neat habit with heart-shaped leaves best grown in clumps; many species are evergreen with leaves turning reddish in winter; very dainty flowers in spring; plant in groups 30–40 cm (12–16 in) apart in sun or shade, in moist soil; 45 × 45 cm (18 × 18 in) (variable).

● Ferns. Many hardy ferns now available; most prefer shade and some are evergreen; best in groups of three or more; 60 cm (2 ft) high (variable).

● Hosta. All hostas love light shade, but also prefer moist soil; striking foliage and white, lilac or pale blue flowers make this plant very popular (especially with slugs!); plant in groups; 60 × 60 cm (24 × 24 in) (variable).

● Lilies. Magnificent growing up through perennials or low shrubs; many are wonderfully scented; about 1.2 m × 60 cm (4 × 2 ft) (variable).

● Primula. Most primulas will thrive in light shade and candelabra primulas are particularly outstanding in moist soil; about 45 × 45 cm (18 × 18 in) (variable).

BULBS

● *Anemone nemerosa* (wood anemone). Pale mixtures of colours in early spring; superb as mass planting under trees and shrubs.

● Colchicum (autumn crocus). Refreshing burst of colour without leaves in autumn.

● Cyclamen. Plant the corms shallowly, in well-drained soil under trees or at the base of a north-facing wall; *C. neapolitanum* flowers in the autumn; *C. coum* in winter and spring.

● Narcissus (daffodil). Familiar sight in spring; always plant in bold clumps for best effect.

● Galanthus (snowdrop). Such an uplifting sight in winter and spring; best in light shade.

● Endymion (bluebell). A natural beauty hard to beat; try for the effect of a sea of bluebells in a woodland setting.

The Shady Garden

Kathy had lived in the house for some time and exhausted all her efforts by making the inside habitable. Unfortunately the garden was last on the list and was desperately in need of attention. A circular gravel area had been attempted but was unsuccessful due to falling leaves and the local cats using it as a giant litter tray!

The garden measured about 7 × 10 m (22 × 32 ft) and was dominated by a beautiful but overpowering oak tree. This caused dense shade, allowing only a few plants to survive. The only other thing in the garden was an old bath-tub!

A gloomy area under a huge oak tree seems an inhospitable place to create a garden.

Design

Kathy and I both decided that we liked the dappled shade that trees create, but agreed that the oak needed thinning out. We decided to change the gravel for timber to discourage the cats and brighten up the area. This would become a wooden, circular, seating area. The bath-tub would become an ornamental focal point.

OPPOSITE *It's amazing what can be done by choosing the right plants for the job and having fun with the design.*

Materials

5 × 2.4 m × 5 × 5 cm (8 ft × 2 × 2 in) timbers (cut into 60 cm (2 ft) lengths then pointed and used as stakes for horizontals)
7 × 3 m × 5 × 8 cm (10 ft × 2 × 3 in) timbers (for the horizontal supports)
18 × 3 m × 15 × 2.5 cm (10 ft × 6 × 1 in) boards (for floor to circle)
6 × 45 × 45 cm (18 × 18 in) stepping stones to lead from back door to circle
paint for bath

Step-by-step

1 **Pruning the oak tree** The first thing to do was to thin the oak tree, carefully. Many of the overlapping stems were removed while the shape of the tree was retained. The garden began to appear much lighter. We used a chainsaw but it would be best to get a professional in to do this if you haven't used one before. Hand saws are fine if you are fit and happy with heights. We used a shredder to reduce the cut-offs to wood chip. This can be composted to form an excellent mulch.

2 **Replacing the gravel with wood** Although gravel can be used to improve drainage on clay soils, the soil here was rich and full of humus. The size of the circle balanced well with the rest of the garden. Short stakes 5 cm (2 in) square were driven into the ground about 45 cm (1½ ft) apart following the inner circumference of the circle. These were left about 8 cm (3 in) proud of the ground. The horizontals, 5 × 8 cm (2 × 3 in) wide were then nailed to the protruding stakes to form the framework for the flooring. All the timber was treated to prevent rotting.

Once the near-circle of horizontal timbers was ready, boards 3 m × 15 cm (10 ft × 6 in) were nailed to them, leaving a 1 cm (½ in) gap between the boards for effect and to help prevent slipping. A circle was then pencilled onto the wood: a nail was placed in the centre, and a 1.5 m (5 ft) length of string with a pencil attached used to draw the circle. The circular shape was cut with an electric handsaw following the pencil line.

3 **The bath-tub** The bath-tub became a feature: we used it to make a pond. The tub was painted an attractive blue with exterior metal paint and the plug hole sealed; we positioned it against the wall that received the most light, so that certain water plants could be grown.

As the 'pool' was filled with water, Cathy placed a clay head she had made on a wooden stool in the bath-tub. The effect was hilarious, as it gave the impression of someone taking a bath al fresco!

A power point nearby allowed a small inexpensive pump to circulate the water. Future maintenance will merely involve removing fallen leaves from the pool. (If you have really deep shade, use artificial plants which look like the real thing under water.)

4 **The plants** A careful selection of plants was used, not merely to give an instant effect, but with thought for future maturity.

The main specimen plants included *Dicksonia* or Tasmanian tree fern, magnificent hardy ferns giving a tropical rainforest feel. They can survive our cold winters, especially in the city. A group of *Hydrangea paniculata* 'Grandiflora' gave brightness and light with their huge panicles of pure white flowers.

The remaining plants were lower growing perennials and shrubs to give interest throughout the year. Variegated ivy and Virginia creeper were planted against the back wall, which would eventually cover the rather dull brickwork.

OPPOSITE *Even the old bath-tub came in useful.*

PLANTS USED FOR THE TV GARDEN

- 6 × *Ajuga reptans* (bugle) (see page 45).
- 6 × *Alchemilla mollis* (lady's mantle) (see page 45).
- 6 × *Bergenia cordata* (see page 45).
- 3 × cornus (dogwood) (see page 42).
- 2 × *Dicksonia* (Tasmanian tree fern). Exotic-looking fern which grows into tree-like proportions in many years; 3–4 m (10–13 ft) × 2 m (6 ft).
- 6 × *Euonymus fortunei* 'Emerald 'n' Gold' (see page 44).
- 3 × ferns (various hardy types) (see page 45).
- 6 × hosta (see page 45).

- 1 × *Phygelius* (Cape figwort). Unusual plant with beautiful nodding, orangey flowers on long stems in summer; 1.2 m × 60 cm (4 × 2 ft).
- 3 × *Hedera helix* ssp. *helix* 'Chicago'. Evergreen, creamy and green variegated foliage to brighten up the back wall.
- 3 × *Viburnum davidii* (see page 44).
- 2 × *Parthenocissus tricuspidata* 'Veitchii' (Virginia creeper) (see page 44).

chapter four

The Water Garden

I have always felt that no garden is really complete without some sort of water feature, be it a fishpond, a natural wildlife pool or a wall-mounted fountain. You don't need a lot of space to introduce water; even on a small patio or in a tiny back yard, a simple recycling millstone fountain, for instance, can be very effective indeed, or just an upturned oak half-barrel.

Water gardening has a long history, from the formal water gardens of the Middle East to the enormous artificial lakes designed and created by Capability Brown. In Brown's case, entire villages had to be relocated if they got in the way of his grand schemes!

Birds love to drink and bathe in shallow water, so this brings another element into the garden. Other wildlife such as frogs, toads and newts need water to breed and will feed on your garden pests.

Children are fascinated by water, so extra care must be taken if you have a young family.

The sight and sound of water add another dimension to the garden.

Even a very shallow pool can be dangerous for kids and so may possibly be best filled with sand or soil for a few years until they grow up. Self-contained, gurgling water features give a great effect and are safe for young children.

Water affects most people in some way: it has a very calming influence – especially useful in this fast-moving, modern world.

There is a misconception that water in the garden needs a lot of maintenance. But a simple well-planted pond, in the right position, should bring years of pleasure and need very little work.

DESIGN

The design of your water feature depends mainly on personal choice and to a large extent on the style of the garden and house.

In a very disciplined, formal garden, a rectangular pool with a paving surround may look superb, but in a more natural-looking garden an irregular pond that looks like it has been created by nature, may be more suitable.

Ornamental bridges really look striking and even a simple flat bridge made of two railway sleepers is very easy to create and gives a great feeling of adventure and fun.

SITE

Always build your pond in a sunny position to get maximum health from your pond plants and wildlife. Never position a pond under trees, or in shade. You will have great difficulty in keeping the water clear of leaves and debris.

DESIGNING FOR FEATURES

Waterfalls and streams

Intricate waterfalls and interconnecting streams, are all achievable, especially if you have a natural bank or slope. Butyl liners make creating these fairly involved schemes far easier and more reliable than old-fashioned concrete. Concrete used over a Butyl liner stream will hide the liner and look natural once moss and algae have taken hold (see Materials and mechanics, page 53–5).

If an area of still water is in some way unsuitable, perhaps because of young children, then a recycling stream or waterfall scheme can be built. The water is pumped back up to the top by using a pump in a sump at the bottom. This can be a relatively small container holding a reservoir of water, then filled with pebbles for safety.

This sort of feature always causes much interest from visitors, who usually wonder where the water is going and where it's coming from!

Remember that any running water will rapidly evaporate, so topping-up the reservoir of a recycling unit or stream regularly, is essential.

Raised pools

Raised pools are a good idea if you are designing a water feature for the elderly, or people with physical disabilities. It brings the water with all its natural beauty to them, reducing the need to bend down too much.

A paving top to the raised pool is useful as a seat and looks visually pleasing.

This type of pool looks great as a semi-circle against a garden wall. A terracotta lion's head expelling water from the wall to the pool below makes it a very strong focal point and is often used in a courtyard or formal design scheme.

Fountains

Self-contained fountains are an excellent focal point, whether they are two- or three-tiered (which look good in a formal garden), or simply a stone urn overflowing with water which collects in a reservoir at the base with cobble stones covering the pump and pipe.

A bubble fountain (see chapter The Patio Garden) is simply a watertight shallow container with a small pump covered by cobbles, which produces a gurgling flow of water.

Barrel ponds

Barrel ponds are another great way to introduce water to a small garden or patio. Oak half-barrels can be used successfully to create a mini-water garden; make sure you choose really non-vigorous plants. *Nymphaea helvola* is a dwarf lily ideal for this situation.

DESIGNING FOR WILDLIFE AND FISH

Remember to allow enough depth in the pool for fish in winter and create shallow ledges for marginal plants. An average pond will support several fish: allow 30 cm square (1 sq ft) of surface area per fish. This will let them grow to their natural size. Introduce them about two months after planting up the pond with oxygenators etc.

Koi carp ponds are very expensive to set up, but I have seen beautiful Koi carp living quite happily for years in a large natural pond with no expensive filtration systems in sight!

Herons can be a problem and have been known to strip an entire pond of fish. A clay drainage pipe is a useful hideaway for fish. Also, an upturned wire shopping basket is a great place for young fish to find refuge from their cannibalistic elders!

Always create a shallow area so that birds can drink and bathe and hedgehogs can climb out easily if they've fallen in.

For a true wildlife pond, fish are perhaps best avoided, or certainly limited, as they feed on eggs and the young of frogs, toads and newts.

Wildlife ponds are generally left to look after themselves, as long as the correct plants have been chosen and the site is in the right place.

In winter, ice can be a problem. Never break the ice forcefully as this can harm any fish beneath. Use a pond heater to keep an area melted to prevent toxic gas build-up.

MATERIALS AND MECHANICS

BUTYL LINERS

This material is now the most popular liner for water gardens, whether it's for a standard pond, or for building a stream or waterfall.

The durability of Butyl is well known. It should last for 20–30 years as long as it is not damaged by a garden fork or sharp rocks. Always use an underfelt between the liner and the soil, as this protects the Butyl from sharp stones, etc. If the pond does spring a leak, however, special repair kits are available, as long as you can find the hole!

For very formal ponds where creases in the liner would be unsightly, specialist firms can mould the liner into any shape required, be it a circle or rectangle. The system is almost like making a made-to-measure suit. I have used this idea when creating a semi-circular pool where the shape would have resulted in too many creases and wastage if a standard liner had been used.

OTHER LINERS

Many other liners are available. It is best to steer clear of thin, cheap materials, as you will probably have to do it all again in five years! New Butyl substitute liners are very flexible and are cheaper than the real thing. They also claim to have a 15-year guarantee, so remember to keep your receipt! The same underfelt procedure must be carried out with all pool lining materials.

Rocks can be used with great effect to hide the edges of a liner pool. Use off-cuts of your liner or old carpet to rest the rock carefully on a wide shallow shelf so that some of the rock is under and some is above the water level. Used round the edges, this method can look very impressive and give the pond a very natural look. Sandstone rocks may crack if used in water, but Westmorland or other hard rock is ideal for this.

Always calculate a large enough liner to allow for the depth of the pond and for plenty spare to enable you to lose the overlap under surrounding rocks or soil. Remember to remove your boots when walking on the liner!

CLAY LINING

If you have a heavy clay subsoil then you may be lucky enough to be able to create a natural pond.

To create a natural pond using imported clay is now a very costly business. The thickness of the clay needs to be at least 30–40 cm (12–16 in) and then 'puddled' which means treading on it for hours until all the air gaps have gone; it should then hold water! Blue clay, particularly, is a wonderful material to use.

Simple streams and bridges create a feeling of adventure. Gravel is useful to disguise unsightly edges.

CONCRETE

Concrete ponds are now almost redundant as they are difficult and expensive to build, but there has been a recent upsurge due to Koi carp enthusiasts.

Concrete blocks are used to create the vertical sides; sand and cement screed is used for the floor and inside. This is then waterproofed using Pondseal or Aquaseal.

A standard garden pond made of concrete, if built properly, can last 20–30 years or more. Another benefit is that they are difficult to damage and a heron will certainly get a shock if it strikes and misses the fish!

Leaking is often a problem if the ground is unstable and cracking can occur. Wire reinforcements should always be used in the concrete during construction to prevent this.

RIGID MOULDS

These were very popular in the 1970s and early 1980s but are less common now. The beauty of them is that all you have to do is dig a hole, place the pool on a sand base, check the levels with a spirit level, then fill in the sides with fine soil or sand. The ledges may need the extra support of rocks or bricks.

It's always best to fill the pond half-way up with water before you start filling in around the sides, as filling it in while empty may lift the mould, or put the levels out.

These ponds, however, can look unnatural, unless you disguise the edges cleverly. Black moulds work best in my opinion.

FILTRATION

To keep a pond crystal clear, a filter system is a good idea, but they can be quite large and difficult to disguise. A biological filtration system can be built into the bottom of the pond and works without fuss and is not visible!

Running water generally keeps a pond fresher and clearer, usually keeping algae and blanket weed at bay. So even a pump without a filter system can often be sufficient.

Barley straw has been proven to keep the water clear, by reducing algae growth.

Oxygenating plants are needed to stop algae growth and are essential for fish (see page 57).

ELECTRICITY AND SAFETY

Always use a circuit-breaker whenever using water in the garden. Unless you are very skilled at DIY it may be better to hire a professional when using electrics in the garden.

PLANTINGS FOR WATER GARDENS

Heavy garden soil is often used over the top of the liner to form a natural bed for plants to take root and grow. This works well, but some water plants may grow too vigorously and get out of hand. Pond plant baskets restrict the growth somewhat and are ideal for maintenance purposes, the plants being easily removed and divided up if needed.

Heavy clay is ideal for your water plants as a compost. This will not float away and is sufficiently heavy to stabilize the planting baskets.

It's best to let pond plants get established for a few weeks before introducing fish to a new pond.

There are four main groups of plants to consider when stocking up your pond. Each does its own particular job in nature and is important for the general health and well-being of your pond. Some of the invasive floating plants can become a nuisance if left unchecked and may smother the surface of the pond, eliminating light and hence life.

DEEP-WATER PLANTS

The term deep water, when referring to man-made ponds, generally means a depth of between 40 and 75 cm (18–30 in). Plants that grow happily here, are as follows:

- *Aponogeton distachyos* (water hawthorn). One of the very few fragrant water plants; bears vanilla-scented flowers throughout the summer on the water surface, amongst flat, oval leaves; ideal planting depth 30–50 cm (12–20 in).
- *Nymphoïdes peltata* (floating heart). Vigorous plant, with yellow, buttercup-like flowers in late summer; good for large ponds, but must be kept in check, or it may take over; ideal planting depth 45–60 cm (18–24 in).
- *Orontium aquaticum* (golden club). Unusual white and yellow flower spikes in late spring; attractive, waxy green leaves that float on the surface of the water; ideal planting depth 30–50 cm (12–20 in).

BOG GARDENS

Bog gardens are a great environment to grow many plants that prefer wet soil but do not necessarily like their roots permanently in water. These boggy areas are naturally found alongside ponds, lakes, streams and rivers and caused by the water overflowing or a high water table. Plants such as astilbe, caltha, hosta, rodgersia, ligularia, *Lobelia cardinalis*, arum lily, primula, mimulus, the giant gunnera, trollius, rheum, filipendula and most of the marginal plants all thrive in these conditions.

- To create a bog garden, simply dig and line a hole about 60 cm (2 ft) deep and as wide as you like. An expensive Butyl liner is not necessary as it doesn't have to be totally watertight.
- Fill the hole with sterilized topsoil (so no liner is visible when planted up) after making a few holes in the liner to take away excess water (leave the bottom 30 cm (12 in) without holes).
- Leave a hosepipe running until the soil is boggy but no water is visible on the surface.
- Plant up and enjoy! Plants will grow vigorously in these perfect conditions and will probably need dividing every two years.

Water lilies for small ponds

● *Nymphaea* × *helvola*. A true miniature, with delicate, soft yellow flowers and maroon-blotched, dark green leaves; ideal depth of water above its roots 15–30 cm (6–12 in).
● *Nymphaea* 'Froebelii'. Dark red, scented flowers and beautiful foliage, make this dwarf water lily a good choice; ideal depth of water above roots 20–30 cm (8–12 in).

Water lilies for medium-sized ponds

● *Nymphaea* 'Conqueror'. Bright red flowers flecked with white over a long period; ideal depth of water above roots 30–45 cm (12–18 in).
● *Nymphaea* 'Marliacea Chromatella'. Soft, primrose yellow flowers and speckled foliage; a reliable and lovely variety; ideal depth of water above roots 30–45 cm (12–18 in).
● *Nymphaea odorata* 'Rose Nymphe'. Deep, rose pink flowers that are sweetly scented; ideal depth of water above roots 30–45 cm (12–18 in).

Water lilies for large ponds

● *Nymphaea alba* 'Attraction'. Beautiful lily bearing enormous deep red flowers, which appear pink on young plants (be patient!); ideal depth of water above roots 60 cm–1.2 m (2–4 ft).
● *Nymphaea alba* 'Gladstoneana'. Exotic-looking lily only for the really large pond; magnificent, pure white flowers can be 30 cm (12 in) across; ideal depth of water above roots 90 cm–1.2 m (3–4 ft).

OXYGENATING WEED

Oxygenating weed is essential in the pond for absorbing carbon dioxide and producing oxygen which fish need to survive; it also provides cover and a place to lay eggs. Waste products from the water which cause algae growth will also be absorbed.

● *Elodea crispa*. Needs deep water; my favourite oxygenator; dark green leaves and tubular growth spread quickly in the pond, so it may need to be kept under control. Ideal depth of water above roots 45–60 cm (18–24 in).
● *Myriophyllum* (water milfoil). Another useful oxygenating weed; light green, feathery foliage favoured by fish for spawning.

MARGINAL PLANTS

These plants are happier in the shallower parts of the pond, needing only a few centimetres of water above their roots. In nature, they grow along the marshy edges of lakes and rivers, where the water levels may rise and fall throughout the year. They provide a home for many pond creatures, and are favoured by dragon-flies as a resting place during their hectic aerobatic displays. Colour is important when making your selection, as many have superb flowers and others have attractive foliage.

● *Butomus umbellatus* (flowering rush). Forms a graceful clump of foliage with pink flowers on long stems; ideal depth of water above roots 15–30 cm (6–12 in).

- *Calla palustris* (bog arum). Pure white flowers in late summer, similar in appearance to the arum lily; glossy, dark green leaves and scrambling stems; ideal depth of water above roots 10–20 cm (4–8 in).
- *Caltha palustris* (marsh marigold). Bright yellow, buttercup flowers in early spring; vigorous plant with large, rounded leaves; ideal depth of water above roots 0–5 cm (boggy soil–2 in).
- *Caltha palustris* 'Flora Plena'. Double yellow flowers; likes shallow water or boggy soil; ideal depth of water above roots 0–5 cm (boggy soil–2 in).
- *Glyceria maxima* var. *variegata* (manna grass). Quickly grows to form an elegant clump of stripy, varying coloured foliage, looking lush all summer; keep in check, as may be invasive; ideal depth of water above roots 15–30 cm (6–12 in).
- *Houttuynia cordata* (chameleon plant). Very colourful leaves of red, yellow and green with herb-like aroma; spreads invasively in boggy soil, but in shallow water in a basket looks wonderful; ideal depth of water above roots 0–10 cm (boggy soil–4 in).
- *Iris laevigata* 'Variegata'. Silvery striped leaves and bright blue flowers; ideal depth of water above roots 0–10 cm (boggy soil–4 in).
- *Iris laevigata* 'Snowdrift'. Bold green leaves with pure white flowers in summer; ideal depth of water above roots 0–10 cm (boggy soil–4 in).
- *Iris versicolor* 'Kermesina'. Unusual deep purple blooms and lush green, strap-like foliage; ideal depth of water above roots 0–30 cm (boggy soil–12 in).

- *Myosotis scorpioïdes* (water forget-me-not). Spreading stems on the surface of the water, bearing pale blue flowers in mid-summer; ideal depth of water above the roots 0–15 cm (boggy soil–6 in).
- *Pontaderia cordata* (pickerel weed). Clump-forming, handsome plant with bold heart-shaped leaves and tall stems of bright blue flowers in late summer; ideal depth of water above roots 5–20 cm (2–8 in).
- *Saururus cernuus* (swamp lily). Attractive foliage colouring nicely in autumn with scented, white, pendulous flowers on tall stems in summer; ideal depth of water above the roots 10–15 cm (4–6 in).
- *Zantedeschia aethiopica* (arum lily). Very exotic-looking plant; even when not in flower, leaves are bold and architectural; magnificent pure white flowers may take some time to appear; ideal depth of water above roots 15–20 cm (6–8 in).

FLOATING PLANTS

These need no soil to grow as they extract their nutrients from the water itself. They are very useful to shade the pond from excessive sun and hence cut down algal growth, as water lilies do. Here are some of the non-invasive species:

- *Eichhornia crassipes* (water hyacinth). This forms a rosette of rounded glossy foliage with leaf stalks swollen with air; not hardy, but looks great in a glass of water on the window sill in the winter; blue flower spikes may appear in a hot summer.

Even tiny gardens can have running water.

● *Hydrocharis morsus-ranae* (frogbit). Neat rosettes of small rounded leaves similar to a miniature water lily; sinks to the bottom in autumn and should reappear on the surface in spring; bears small three-petalled flowers through the summer.

● *Stratiotes aloïdes* (water soldier). My favourite floating plant with bold star-like leaves looking superb throughout the summer; sinks to the safety of the deeper water for the duration of the winter; small white flowers appear in summer.

The Water Garden

A modest, suburban garden in the heart of Walthamstow isn't, I suppose, the natural home of a rushing stream and a large pond, but that is exactly what Peter and Fiona wanted. They had always dreamt of something really bold and eccentric, so a babbling brook reminiscent of the Scottish Highlands was the order of the day.

Design

Standing together on the patio, we all agreed that the pond and stream feature needed to be close to the house, where it would be seen and appreciated. We were keen to do something quite wacky and original and decided to use a bridge to cross from the patio to the lawn!

Materials

Butyl liner, 5 × 3 m (16 × 10 ft)
underfelt, 5 × 3 m (16 × 10 ft)
2 tons Westmorland rock
3 × moulded stream sections about
1 m × 80 cm (3 × 2½ ft)
1 × pump and length of pipe
1 × circuit-breaker
1 × oak bridge, 2.5 m × 80 cm
(8 × 2½ ft) wide

The starting point for the stream and water-fall was high on the garden wall, down three tiers, finally reaching the pond, and pumped back up again. Butyl seemed our best choice for a liner, as we wanted an irregularly shaped pond with ledges for marginals and we needed it deep enough for water lilies.

The stream was created using three separate pre-moulded sections, made from a fibreglass and cement mix. Westmorland rock was to be our mountainside substitute.

Step-by-step

1 **Preparing the hole for the pond** The shape and size of the pond was designed using the hosepipe trick: we tried out various shapes, the final form was agreed upon and marked with a spade before being dug out.

The soil was quite moist and care was taken not to cause the sides to collapse, especially where the shelves were going. The top one of these needed to be about 15–20 cm (6–8 in) below the final water level. As the hole was being dug, a board was laid across it and a tape measure used to check the depths of the pond from the board. The deepest part needed to be at least 60 cm (2 ft) if fish were to be kept safely. A spirit level was also used on the board to check that the edges of the pond were level; otherwise water would leak out of the lowest point when the pond was full.

2 **Lining the pond** Underfelt material was used to line the hole and protect the Butyl from sharp objects. Then the Butyl was spread out and moulded into the cavity. The excess liner was cut off, leaving at least 45 cm (18 in) as an overlap. This was buried in the soil and under rocks. The cut-offs came in handy when rocks were being laid on the liner in the water itself. A hose was used to fill the new pond with water.

3 **The waterfall** Three moulded stream units were used to create the waterfall. These are made from a fibreglass and concrete combination and look very realistic, especially when they have weathered a bit. Westmorland rockery stone was used in and around the pond, as well as to build up the sides of the waterfall. This formed an attractive retaining wall, which contained the soil and streams.

The first stream section was placed on a bed of compressed soil, so that its lip was 20 cm (8 in) over the main pool. This would help

The unlikely site before the transformation.

create the desired sound of the waterfall and look good; the other two falls would add further to the effect.

The soil was then built up behind and around it and firmed down to prevent subsidence. The next section was then placed behind the first, so that its lip was 15 cm (6 in) above the lower stream. Exactly the same procedure was carried out for the third and final stream section which finished our waterfall.

RIGHT AND BELOW *The stream sections and rock blend in successfully.*

Sphagnum moss was pushed between the streams and the rocks to blend the two materials together, so that the whole thing looked completely natural. A pipe was positioned into the top stream and buried under the soil to lead down into the main pond. This was attached to a powerful pond pump which created the rushing water feature.

4 **The plants** The lilies were lowered into the water in baskets with two pieces of string threaded through each side. With one person either side of the pond holding a string, the lilies were lowered carefully into position. The string was then simply pulled out through one side of the basket. This method is very useful if plants are to be placed in a wide pool with deep water.

The marginal plants, chosen for maximum effect throughout the summer, were placed in their baskets on the shelves. A few slow-growing shrubs and a blue juniper (which would eventually hang into the water) were planted near the waterfall. Some perennials went in alongside the pond.

5 **The bridge** We chose a beautiful, oak, hump-back bridge which looked really good once in place. It had to be wide enough because this was the only access from the patio to the rest of the garden.

When we switched the pump on (which was connected to a circuit-breaker at the mains), the effect was tremendous: a real torrent of water gushed down the waterfall and into the pond below. Peter and Fiona were delighted.

PLANTS USED FOR THE TV GARDEN

- *Aponogeton distachyos* (water hawthorn) (see page 56).
- *Elodea crispa* (oxygenating weed) (see page 57).
- *Houttuynia cordata* (chamaeleon plant) (see page 58).
- *Iris laevigata* (see page 58).
- *Nymphaea* 'Ellisiana' (water lily). Beautiful lily with carmine red flowers and attractive leaves; not too vigorous for a medium-sized pond.
- *Nymphaea* 'Marliacea Albida' (water lily). Large, scented, white flowers ideal for medium-sized ponds.
- *Pontaderia cordata* (pickerel weed) (see page 58).
- *Saururus cernuus* (swamp lily) (see page 58).

Nymphaea *'Ellisiana' will flower for months.*

chapter five

The Low-maintenance Garden

Many people imagine gardening to be all hard work with very little pleasure. This doesn't have to be the case, if a low maintenance scheme is created.

We often adopt gardens that require a lot of maintaining, be it tying up or deadheading perennial plants, spraying roses, pruning trees and worst of all *weeding*! Most of us have limited time available for these 'chores' and would sooner spend our free time enjoying the garden, rather than toiling in it!

The type of high-maintenance gardening involving mass bedding schemes which was well known in the past, when labour was cheap, is still practised with great effect by many towns around the country, such as Brighton, Blackpool, Eastbourne and Worthing. Colourful as they are, this is very labour-intensive, and although still popular in many private gardens, there are people who loathe dealing with seasonal bedding plants and weeding, which can seem to be never-ending tasks. A low-maintenance garden is thus ideal for our modern, fast-moving society where the prospect of slaving in the garden can be the last straw after a hard week at the office. We all want something that looks good, but don't necessarily want to spend our valuable free time keeping it that way.

DESIGN

If you are starting from scratch, it is far easier to create a low-maintenance garden because you can design the hard landscape and select the right plants that need minimal attention. An established garden, however, will almost certainly contain plants that may need attention, and borders that may be wide and unmanageable.

Large lawn areas may be relatively easy to look after, compared with herbaceous beds for instance, but for a small garden, lawns can be a nuisance and may be better if converted into paving, gravel or low-maintenance shrubs.

Borders wider than 1 m (3 ft) are difficult to weed and maintain, as you may have to step into them to reach certain plants, making garden maintenance unenjoyable. Raised beds can be a joy to work, particularly for older people (see page 76–7).

A small tree positioned in a particular place can give valuable shade in summer to a very hot, dry border, meaning less watering. Choosing ornamental or fruit trees on a dwarf root stock will require little or no pruning, which is ideal for restricted space and easy to look after.

Access around the garden is very important too, and if borders are edged with paths, grass does not encroach into them and weeding or planting can be carried out from 'dry land', even in winter. The less hassle gardening involves, the more it can be enjoyed.

An irrigation system (see page 69–70) is another great way to solve the problem of spending too much time and effort in the garden. Automatic timers will operate the water outlets whether they are sprays or drips (used for hanging baskets), and come on at predetermined times. Fertilizer can be added to the system in order to feed the plants as well – what could be easier?

THINGS TO AVOID

- Wide beds are difficult to maintain, unless cleverly planted with ground cover or mulched.
- Roses are high-maintenance plants if you want to keep them healthy.
- Bedding plants are great 'fillers' between shrubs, or in pots and baskets, but beds dedicated to bedding plants are labour-intensive, as they are so seasonal.
- Herbaceous perennials can need a lot of maintenance, unless you go for the low, bushy species that don't require tying up.
- Over-planting is not the solution to a low-maintenance garden, as the plants compete for light and tend to become overgrown; they will require constant pruning.
- Never plant new plants in an area where they are not suited, e.g. planting hydrangeas, which need plenty of moisture, in a dry, sunny spot will increase the amount of watering you will have to do.

IDEAS FOR LOW-MAINTENANCE GARDENS

- Raised beds: plants and weeds can be easily reached making gardening less back breaking (see page 76–7). Use ericaceous compost if you want to grow lime-haters such as rhododendrons.
- Use paving instead of lawn. Stand easily maintained containers on the paving for colourful spots. (See chapter The Patio Garden.)

- Make a water feature with a millstone or a bubble fountain. (See chapter The Water Garden.)
- Use more hard landscaping than usual.
- Keep weeds down by use of mulching (page 67–9) and ground-cover plants (page 73–5).

DEALING WITH WEEDS

● Weedkillers are available that prevent weed seedlings from germinating and keep the bare soil between shrubs weed-free all season! (Enquire at your local garden centre.)

● Be sure to remove perennial weeds before planting up a bed, as things like bindweed and ground elder are virtually impossible to eradicate in an established border.

● Choosing ground-cover plants in the design, to help prevent weed growth, is a great way to cut down on work and can be applied to an established garden. Groups of the same type of plant are recommended to form a good cover and will also look more effective.

● Hoeing regularly is a superb way of preventing seedlings from getting a foothold and once you get the hang of it, is very relaxing and an effective method of weed control. It also helps to retain moisture in the soil by forming a tilth.

● Finally, mulching is one of the most effective weed suppressors. (See section below on mulching.)

OPPOSITE *Frost-proof bricks are an attractive low-maintenance surface and keeping flower beds narrow also makes sense.*

RIGHT *Pine bark chippings make an excellent mulch and enhance flower and foliage colour.*

MULCHING

This is the term used to describe the covering of the soil with a man-made or natural material to help prevent weed growth and to cut down on evaporation from the soil. Even old carpets can be used. A mulch can also be an attractive background for plants which helps them to look their best.

Never mulch before perennial weeds have been removed, unless you are using landscape fibre or polythene.

MAN-MADE MULCHES

Polythene sheeting

This has been used for years. It needs to be black to prevent the light and thus plant growth.

Disadvantages are that it looks unsightly, is easily damaged, can blow away unless secured, does not allow moisture into the soil and may cause flooding elsewhere.

Advantages are that it is cheap to buy, keeps perennial weeds at bay if roots are in soil and can be disguised with bark or gravel (fork holes allow some rain to get in).

Recycled paper mulch

This is a relatively new concept that has a future more in the commercial growers' market. For the garden, it may look unsightly, but for large landscaping schemes, it makes good sense.

Disadvantages are that it looks unsightly, needs to be secured and has only a limited life-span.

Advantages are that it is good value, it decomposes to enrich the soil in two to three years (when plants should be established), and it can be dug into the soil after the first season as a soil improver.

Landscape fibre

I use landscape fibre under gravel, or in some cases bark. It's made of strong nylon fibres that allow the soil to breathe, but prevent weeds growing through indefinitely.

Disadvantages are that it is pretty expensive, looks unsightly unless covered and it needs securing down.

Advantages are that it allows in air and rain, it's very strong, lasts indefinitely, even the toughest weeds cannot penetrate it and it's good as a base for gravel or stone chippings to prevent soil mixing in.

NATURAL MULCHES

Bark

This is the most popular mulching material these days. The large chunky pieces are far better used on large landscaping schemes as they just don't look right with the more delicate or small-leaved garden plants and shrubs. The finer bark chippings are much more suited here as is the fine shredded bark which can be dug into the soil as a conditioner as well (unlike the others). There is no point using bark unless you apply it no less than 3 cm (1¼ in) deep, or light will penetrate it allowing seedlings to germinate and grow. Remember bark will not stop perennial weeds from growing through if roots are left in (unless you use landscape fibre underneath).

Disadvantages are that it is expensive by the bag (but by the lorry load it is far cheaper), insects use it to hibernate and breed, the finer bark is often displaced by blackbirds searching for food and big pieces look wrong with some plants.

Advantages are that it looks very effective as a foil for plants, especially the dark brown bark, and it's lightweight, easy to apply and readily available, it's an organic material, a good insulator, usually a neutral pH and bark chippings take years to break down (except the shredded type).

Mushroom compost

This is now very popular and it is relatively cheap, a by-product of the mushroom industry. It breaks down after a couple of years, enriching the soil.

Disadvantages are that it has a high pH, so is not recommended for acid-loving plants such as rhododendrons, it must be topped up periodically, you may introduce mushrooms to your garden and it needs to be at least 5 cm (2 in) deep.

Advantages are that it is relatively cheap, a good soil conditioner, looks good as a dark base to plants, a good insulator, good for soil organisms and easy to apply.

Gravel

This must be used on top of landscape fibre or polythene or it will eventually mix with the earth (unless you apply it thickly enough).

Disadvantages are that it is heavy and may be expensive, the light colour may not show off plants to their best potential, it can be dazzling in sun and cats use it like cat litter.

Advantages are that it will not blow away, is sterile and is not favoured by pests, is good for Mediterranean schemes, looks clean and neat and lasts forever.

Cocoa shell

This is becoming more popular as it is dark brown and the pieces are small and even sized. After a few weeks it 'binds' together as it breaks down. It needs to be at least 3–5 cm (1½–2 in) deep.

Disadvantages are that it may blow about until it 'binds' together, birds often disturb it in search of food, it breaks down after a time, is quite expensive and smells of chocolate (no good if you're on a diet!).

Advantages are that it is lightweight and easy to apply, it smells nice to some people, it looks good, eventually makes a good soil conditioner, is organic and a good insulator.

Fypro

This is a new material that is the by-product of the rape seed industry. It has fared well in recent trials and lasts for years as an effective mulch.

Disadvantages are that it is not yet readily available across the country and birds disturb it searching for food.

Advantages are that it looks great as very fine pieces, can be used as soil conditioner, is organic and a waste material, relatively good value, a good insulator and easy to apply.

IRRIGATION

POP-UP SPRINKLERS

These are unobtrusive and very effective. They work by water pressure which forces the sprinklers up before they expel water. Ideal for large lawns where the pipework is hidden underneath and the sprinklers disappear from view once finished, allowing the mower to pass over. If fixed to a timer, you don't even have to switch it on! The system also works well in borders, but note that tall, bushy shrubs will block the spray.

DRIP IRRIGATION

This is mainly used for tubs and hanging baskets. It involves a network of thin pipes leading from a main pipe and then to the water tap. A constant supply of water is slowly released. The system can be set by an electronic timer.

THE LEAKY PIPE SYSTEM

This is a great way to get the water directly to the roots. Porous rubber pipes are buried around the garden amongst plants and shrubs constantly releasing water right where they need it most. This is totally undetectable and prevents wastage through evaporation from the surface.

PLANTINGS FOR LOW-MAINTENANCE GARDENS

There are many types of plants which will aid in smothering weeds or need little attention in themselves. Some points to note:

- Choose plants and shrubs that need little or no pruning and minimum aftercare, for example, dwarf pines and miniature hebes.
- Choosing drought-tolerant plants will cut down watering requirements.
- Silver and fleshy-leaved plants and shrubs rarely need watering, such as santolina and sedum.
- Evergreen shrubs are usually good to smother weed growth by cutting out the light.
- A growth retardant is available to spray on hedges such as privet, to slow down their growth, cutting down pruning to once a year!
- If you particularly want roses, the shrub roses need less pruning and are often quite tolerant to diseases, but they do normally grow quite large. Disease-resistant strains of patio roses and 'County' roses are also less prone to disease and need less pruning.

ALPINES

Most rockery plants are generally low-maintenance and will stay short and dense, preventing weed seedlings from germinating. You may have to trim them back after flowering to keep them bushy, e.g. helianthemum and iberis, but little or no other care is needed.

Plant alpines in sun, in groups of the same type at the base of shrubs, about 20–30 cm (8–12 in) apart, for the best effect. (See chapter The Rock Garden for more details.)

PERENNIAL PLANTS

Low-level perennials are an excellent form of ground cover at the base of trees and shrubs. Many have luxuriant foliage, others have showy flowers and some are even evergreen! Their foliage often complements the shrubs above them; try the silver-leafed anaphalis with the purple cotinus bush. As with the alpine plants, these too, are best planted in groups of three or more to create the best effect and to smother out weeds. Tall, flowering perennials generally need more maintenance.

- *Alchemilla mollis* (lady's mantle). (See page 45.)
- *Anaphalis triplinervis.* Silver-leaved, clump-forming plant with white 'everlasting' flowers from mid-summer onwards; sunny site; plant in groups 30–40 cm (12–16 in) apart; 38 × 45 cm (15 × 18 in) in 3 years.

Many plants need very little attention and gravel makes an effective mulch to control the weeds.

● *Artemisia* 'Powis Castle'. An excellent silver-leaved plant/shrub which acts as a foil for other flowers or purple leaf colour; cut back each spring to keep bushy; best planted in sun in well-drained or dryish soil; plant in groups 45 cm (1½ ft) apart; 60 × 75 cm (2 × 2½ ft) if cut back annually.

● *Astilbe chinensis* 'Pumila'. Loves moist soil, so often seen near water (see page 45). It makes a fine clump of foliage with mauve-pink flowers in mid- to late summer; plant in groups 30–40 cm (12–16 in) apart in sun or light shade; 45 × 45 cm (18 × 18 in) in 3 years.

● Bergenia. Plant in groups 30–40 cm (12–16 in) apart in sun or shade (see page 45).

● *Convallaria majalis* (lily-of-the-valley). Very tough ground-cover plant, often thriving in poor soil under trees; beautifully scented flowers in spring; sometimes unwilling to grow in certain places; plant in groups 30 cm (12 in) apart in sun or shade; 23 × 30 cm (9 × 12 in) in 3 years.

● Epimedium. (See page 45.)

● Euphorbia. Some varieties grow too tall as ground cover, but all will tolerate the dry soil at the base of shrubs; they exude a milky liquid when damaged, which can be an irritant; many have architectural evergreen leaves; plant in groups 45 cm (18 in) apart in full sun, or semi-shade; *E. robiae* is good in shade under trees and has dark evergreen leaves, low-spreading habit and limey-green flowers in spring; 45 × 45 cm (18 × 18 in) in 3 years.

● Geranium. Not to be confused with the pelargonium family; hardy geraniums are a first-class ground cover under shrubs or trees, smothering out weed seedlings; one of my favourites is *G. endressii*, with its low-spreading habit; evergreen leaves and pretty pink flowers; plant in groups 30 cm (12 in) apart in sun or semi-shade; 45 × 50 cm (18 × 20 in) in 3 years.

● Helleborus. Most species have dark, evergreen leaves with limey-green flowers in winter/spring; poisonous if eaten; *H. niger* (Christmas rose) is lower growing with large white blooms in winter; plant in groups 30–40 cm (12–16 in) apart in sun or shade; 30 × 40 cm (12 × 16 in) in 3 years (*H. niger*).

● Heuchera. Rounded, evergreen leaves and clump-forming habit; tall stems of numerous tiny bell-shaped pink or red flowers in summer; *H.* 'Palace Purple' has dark purple leaves which is a valuable colour contrast amongst green, silver or golden foliage; plant in groups 30–40 cm (12–16 in) apart in sun or semi-shade; 45 × 45 cm (18 × 18 in) in 3 years.

● Hosta. *H.* 'Francis Williams' is a favourite; gold-edged large bluey leaves with lilac/white flowers in summer; plant in groups 30–40 cm (12–16 in) apart in moist soil in sun or shade; (see page 45). 60 × 45 cm (24 × 18 in).

● *Lamium maculatum* 'Beacon Silver'. Silver and green variegated evergreen leaves; very low ground cover in shady or sunny moist position; plant 30 cm (12 in) apart; 23 × 45 cm (9 × 18 in) in 3 years.

● Penstemon. Not strictly a ground-cover plant, but its bushy habit and evergreen leaves blot out the bare soil at the base of shrubs especially in a sunny, dry position; very long flowering period; plant in groups 30–40 cm (12–16 in) apart in sun.

● Polygonum. Very tough, rapidly spreading plant, some bearing pink, others red flower spikes in summer and autumn; *P. bistorta* 'Superbum' (now known as *Persicaria bistorta* 'Superbum') is excellent ground cover with its pink spikes appearing in mid-summer; *P. affine* (now *Persicaria affinis*) is much lower growing, with red flower spikes over a long period in summer to autumn; plant 30–40 cm (12–16 in) apart in more or less any soil, in sun or semi-shade; 23 × 45 cm (9 × 18 in) in 3 years.

● *Salvia purpurea* (purple sage). Aromatic, evergreen leaves and wide-spreading growth; good ground cover at the base of Mediterranean shrubs; *S. officinalis* 'Tricolor' is a beautiful multicoloured variety; plant in groups 30–40 cm (12–16 in) apart in sunny, well-drained spot; prune half-way back each April; 30 × 60 cm (12 × 24 in).

● Tellima. Hardy, evergreen ground cover with bold, rounded leaves and creamy bell-like flower sprays on tall stems; good under trees and shrubs; plant in groups 30–40 cm (12–16 in) apart in sun or semi-shade; 45 × 45 cm (18 × 18 in) in 3 years.

GRASSES

● Carex. Attractive creamy and green striped foliage arching down to the ground and forming neat clumps; excellent with tidy evergreens such as hebe or cistus, or in containers; best planted in groups of three or more, in sun or semi-shade; 23 × 30 cm (9 × 12 in) in 3 years.

● *Festuca glauca*. Striking blue grass forming spiky clumps 30 cm (12 in) high; very effective with other grass-like plants or with Mediterranean shrubs; plant in groups 30 cm (12 in) apart in sun; good in containers; 23 × 30 cm (9 × 12 in) in 3 years.

● *Hakonechloa macra* 'Aureola'. Superb spreading grass with bright golden foliage; needs moist soil to do well; effective in front of purple or dark green shrubs; plant in groups 30–40 cm (12–16 in) apart in sun or semi-shade; good in containers; 30 × 46 cm (12 × 18 in) in 3 years.

● Molinia. Another beautiful grass; variegated form has soft golden stripy leaves; plant 30 cm (12 in) apart in sun or semi-shade; good in containers; 30 × 30 cm (12 × 12 in) in 3 years.

GROUND-COVER EVERGREEN SHRUBS

● *Ceanothus repens* (Californian lilac). The prostrate form is evergreen and bears a profusion of powder-blue flowers in summer; may grow into a large mound, unless selectively pruned in mid-summer; plant in sun; 60 cm × 1.2 m (2 × 4 ft) in 3 years.

● *Cistus decumbens* – low-growing evergreen with white poppy-like flowers in summer; needs sunny, well-drained site; 45 × 60 cm (18 in × 2 ft) in 3 years.

● *Cotoneaster dammerii*. (See page 44.) *C. × suecicus* 'Skogholm' is more rampant growing – 60 cm × 1.2 m (2 × 3 ft 8 in) in 3 years.

● Euonymus. (See page 44.)

- Hebe. All hebes are ideal for a sunny position and dry soil; small-leaved varieties are tougher; *H. subalpina* tough, bushy, evergreen with light-green dense foliage and white flowers in summer; mound-forming habit; plant 40 cm (16 in) apart in sunny, well-drained or dry site; *H. pinguifolia* 'Pagei' has silvery leaves and a prostrate habit, hugging the ground; covered in white flowers in spring to summer; plant in groups 30–40 cm (12–16 in) apart; 10 × 45 cm (4 × 18 in) in 3 years.
- Hedera – ivies are superb ground cover in sun or shade. Small-leaved varieties are less invasive; 15 × 60 cm (6 in × 2 ft).
- *Hypericum calycinum*. Extremely invasive, but very effective ground cover in shade with huge yellow flowers and evergreen leaves; only for certain situations such as under trees or in their own bed; 30 × 45 cm (12 × 18 in) in 3 years.
- *Ilex crenata* 'Little Gem'. This is a holly, but you would never think so, golden, thornless leaves appear even brighter in winter; low-spreading habit; plant 40 cm (16 in) apart in sun or semi-shade; very hardy; 30 × 45 cm (12 × 18 in) in 3 years.
- Lavandula (lavender). Not a true ground-cover shrub, but does the job admirably if planted in front of shrubs in a sunny, well-drained or dry position; *L. angustifolia* 'Hidcote' is dark blue, or *L. a.* 'Munstead Dwarf' lighter blue, are the best choices; plant 40 cm (16 in) apart; excellent as an aromatic edging to path; prune every spring to keep bushy; *L. a.* 'Munstead Dwarf' 30 × 45 cm (12 × 18 in) if pruned annually.

- *Lonicera pileata*. (See page 44.)
- Pachysandra. This is not that widely grown, but is a worthy ground-cover plant and is good in shade; dark green leathery leaves and creeping habit; white flowers appear in spring; not for limey soil; plant 40 cm (16 in) apart; 23 × 40 cm (9 × 16 in) in 3 years.
- *Prunus laurocerasus* 'Zabeliana' and *P. l.* 'Otto Luyken'. Both good in shade and spread well; evergreen, shiny leaves and creamy white flower spikes in early summer; best in groups 60–90 cm (2–3 ft) apart; 60 × 90 cm (2 × 3 ft) in 3 years; (see also page 44).
- Roses (ground-cover 'County' roses). Dense, spreading growth, with almost evergreen leaves; various colours available, my favourite being 'Hertfordshire' which is deep cerise pink; no spraying needed, good for sunny banks; plant in groups 50 cm (20 in) apart; 30 × 60 cm (12 × 24 in) in 3 years.
- *Rubus calycinoïdes* (cultivated blackberry). Flat, spreading growth, very vigorous and tolerant; grows well in shade; evergreen leaves, white flowers, red fruits; plant 60–75 cm (2–2½ ft) apart; good for covering banks or under trees; invasive; 15 × 75 cm (6 × 30 in) in 3 years.
- Santolina (cotton lavender). Dense, mound-forming evergreen (silver); not strictly a ground-cover plant but like the lavender will do a great job if planted in groups; it should be cut back hard each spring, or will become open and woody in the centre; plant 30–40 cm (12–16 in) apart in a sunny, well-drained or dry position; good as a foil for blue flowers; 30 × 45 cm (12 × 18 in) if pruned annually.

- Sarcococca (Christmas box). Readily available but is not often seen in private gardens; narrow, glossy, evergreen leaves and dense suckering habit make it good ground cover; richly perfumed white flowers appear in winter followed by black berries; quite slow to establish; plant in groups 30–40 cm (12–16 in) apart in humus-rich soil; good in shade; 30 × 40 cm (12 × 16 in) in 3 years.
- Skimmia. Male plants bear pinky red buds throughout winter, opening to scented white flowers in spring; females have less showy flowers but bright red berries in autumn and winter; both grow about 45 × 45 cm (18 × 18 in) in 3 years; *S. japonica* 'Rubella' is a particularly good plant. Best in groups of 3 or more, 45 cm (18 in) apart.
- *Viburnum davidii*. Plant in groups 45 cm (1½ ft) apart in sun or shade; (see page 49).
- *Vinca* (periwinkle) (see page 44).

LOW-MAINTENANCE CLIMBERS

- Hedera (ivy). Small-leaved varieties are less invasive; 1.5 m × 90 cm (5 × 3 ft) in 3 years.
- *Hydrangea petiolaris*. (See page 44.)
- *Lonicera halliana* (evergreen honeysuckle). Lush green foliage; creamy yellow, scented flowers from mid- to late summer; 1.8 × 1.8 m (6 × 6 ft) in 3 years.
- *Parthenocissus tricuspidata* 'Veitchii'. (See page 44.)

GROUND-COVER CONIFERS

- *Juniperus sabina* 'Tamariscifolia'. Beautifully layered, spreading habit, vigorous growth; dark greeny-grey foliage; sun or semi-shade; good in dry soil; 30 × 75 cm (12 in × 2½ ft) in 3 years.
- *Juniperus squamata* 'Blue Carpet'. Flat, spreading habit; bright blue foliage; sun, good in dry soil; 23 × 90 cm (9 in × 3 ft) in 3 years.
- *Juniperus communis* 'Repanda'. Very flat habit; dark green foliage; good for limited space as less vigorous than others; sun or semi-shade; good in dry soil; 5 × 60 cm (2 in × 2 ft) in 3 years.
- *Juniperus × media* 'Old Gold'. Bright golden yellow foliage and spreading habit, becoming quite large in time; best in sun, good in dry soil; 60 × 90 cm (2–3 ft) in 3 years.
- *Microbiota decussens*. One to impress your neighbours with, this unusual conifer grows close to the ground and turns from deep green in summer, to coppery-purple in winter; 5 × 60 cm (2 in × 2 ft) in 3 years.

Slow-growing upright conifers are ideal for a low-maintenance garden as they require no pruning and little watering (unless in containers).

The Low-maintenance Garden

Dolly Dear and her husband had always taken care of their small garden in Essex, but when Len suffered a stroke a few years back the garden became too much for Dolly to cope with on her own and she just let it go.

Design

A beautiful, but enormous, hydrangea was making access difficult and needed to be moved. A philadelphus (mock orange), one of the old vigorous varieties although it had been cut back a couple of years ago, was far too large and the roses that were once Dolly's pride and joy, were thin and weak and covered in black spot and mildew – not good for a low-maintenance garden!

Materials

17 × 3 m × 15 cm (10 ft × 6 in) treated gravel boards
10 × 1.8 m × 5 cm (6 ft × 2 in) square posts
10 m (32 ft) landscape fibre 2 m (6 ft) wide
30 × 40 kg (90 lb) bags of stone chippings
Hammerite paint
10 m (32 ft) polythene sheeting
1 m (3 ft) wide
3 × 1.8 × 1.2 m (6 × 4 ft) trellis panels
4 × 1.8 m × 5 cm (6 ft × 2 in) square posts

The lawn area was small, weedy, a nuisance to cut and Dolly wanted this converted into something less time-consuming. A low rusty wire fence defined the boundary with a good view beyond which Dolly and Len wanted to retain.

We decided to make raised beds which are so much easier for elderly people to work with.

Step-by-step

1 Ground preparation The unwanted mock orange was cut down to the ground and the chemical SBK was used to kill the roots. (This is not harmful to the soil.)

The old roses and other shrubs were also removed. The lawn area was left until later so that it did not end up like a bog and be difficult to work from.

2 The trellis Three large trellis panels were used to give a sense of privacy at the boundary. These still allowed a view through and did not cut out the light.

3 The raised beds We used 15 cm (6 in) wide pressure-treated gravel boards for our raised beds. Once the width of 40 cm (16 in) was determined, 5 cm (2 in) square stakes were hammered into the ground as supports, to

Not exactly a low-maintenance garden.

which the boards were nailed. We checked with Dolly that the height was right for her to reach easily, in this case mostly three boards high.

Once built, the base of the 'boxed' raised beds were covered with black plastic to prevent weeds growing up from the ground.

We filled in with sterilized topsoil, firming it down as we went to prevent too much settling later on. (There is nothing worse than a raised bed with soil and plants that sit 5 cm (2 in) or more below the top.)

4 **The plants** All the plants we used were easy to grow and none grew too fast, nor needed much attention (except watering until established). The hydrangea was replanted in place of the mock orange and a 'Zebrina'

conifer was planted against the side fence to screen off the neighbours' shed. Most of the shrubs were dwarf evergreens with dwarf asters and mini-chrysanthemums to give some instant, short-term colour.

5 **The gravel** There was little left of the lawn by this time, so we merely covered the area with landscape fibre. Beige-coloured stone chippings were used as our new surface which worked well and were not too dazzling.

The only maintenance needed was to remove fallen leaves in autumn and because the stones are larger than gravel, the area shouldn't attract the local cats. (Leaves can be quickly gathered with garden vacuums.)

6 **The railings** The stark metal hand-rail along the path, was painted with a dark blue Hammerite paint, which transformed it beautifully.

PLANTS USED FOR THE TV GARDEN

● 6 × aster (dwarf). More resistant to mildew than its larger relatives; grows best in sun in well-drained soil; flowers in late summer to autumn; 30–40 × 30–40 cm (12–16 in × 12–16 in).

● 1 × *Chamaecyparis lawsoniana* 'Ellwood's Pillar' (see page 29).

● 1 × *Chamaecyparis pisifera* 'Nana' (see page 33).

● 1 × *Chamaecyparis lawsoniana* 'Ellwood's Gold' (see page 29).

● 1 × halimiocistus. Sun-loving plant with fleshy grey-green leaves; large bright yellow flowers with red blotches; 60 × 60 cm (2 × 2 ft) in 3 years.

● 1 × *Hebe buxifolia* 'Nana'. Evergreen; small, glossy leaves and neat, rounded habit; white flowers in spring to early summer; 30 × 45 cm (12 × 18 in).

● 1 × *Hebe* 'Carl Teschner'. Evergreen; very low-growing plant; violet-blue flowers in mid-summer; 15 × 45 cm (6 × 18 in).

● 1 × *Hebe pimeleoïdes* 'Quicksilver'.

● 3 × *Leucothoë* 'Scarletta'. Dark green leaves turning deep red in autumn and winter; 40 × 46 cm (16 × 18 in) in 3 years.

● 15 × mini-chrysanthemums. Bedding plants, used as seasonal colour; available from July onwards.

● 3 × *Skimmia japonica* 'Rubella' (see page 75).

● 1 × *Thuja occidentalis* 'Golden Globe' (see page 33).

● 1 × *Thuja occidentalis* 'Sunkist'. Conical habit; golden foliage, changing to an orangy colour in autumn to winter; 90 × 60 cm (3 × 2 ft) in 10 years.

● 1 × *Thuja plicata* 'Zebrina'. Golden-flecked foliage; dense habit (good for screening); 3 × 1.2 m (9 × 4 ft) in 10 years, if unpruned.

● 3 × pernettya. Small prickly evergreen leaves; tiny bell-like flowers in summer, forming striking berries for autumn and winter; best in acid soil; 60 × 60 cm (2 × 2 ft).

● *Santolina chamaecyparissus* (see page 74).

● 1 × dwarf rhododendron (see page 117).

OPPOSITE AND BELOW *Raised beds make life much easier and gravel boards are cheap and easy to use.*

chapter six

The Neglected Garden

Whether you've just moved into a new home and adopted a wilderness, or whether your own garden has just grown out of control over the years, this chapter is for you.

Personally, I love to tackle a really neglected garden, where everything is overgrown. To me it's the ultimate gardening challenge and often not quite as daunting or costly a task as it may at first appear.

My first advice is, not to panic or make any hasty decisions on the fate of trees, shrubs and plants. Most can be rejuvenated after careful pruning and patience, although some may never be restored to their former glory and might need removing.

If you're not an expert on identifying trees and shrubs, then always get help from a knowledgeable gardener. They should be able to advise you on which plants are beyond hope and which are worth keeping. Take your time to assess the situation carefully, so that a proper plan of action can be worked out before you consider attacking your garden. Remember that five minutes with a chainsaw or mechanical digger can do untold damage to beautiful trees and shrubs that often demand a much gentler and considerate approach. (See pruning section, page 81–5 and 87.)

It may be a good idea to visit some gardens that have been renovated. One such public garden is the Lost Garden of Heligan in Mevagissey, Cornwall. Here, after 60 years of neglect, a dedicated team has brought back to life manmade streams and waterfalls, tree ferns, a Victorian walled garden and a greenhouse for pine-apples.

I once discovered a turn-of-the-century sunken garden hidden by undergrowth, which would have been ruined if mechanical diggers had been used initially, so always take your time to properly assess the site.

DESIGN

Restoring a neglected garden back to its former glory can be a very rewarding experience.

A total rejuvenation may not always be what is required. Sometimes a slightly overgrown-looking garden may be preferred. As long as some order is maintained, so that you have access around the garden, this sort of natural design can work brilliantly. Mature trees and shrubs can be thinned out and pruned so that they still maintain that untamed look (not described in most books!); this can give the garden a mysterious, yet romantic, atmosphere.

Assess the site carefully and decide what to keep and what to prune or discard. This may also help you decide upon a focal point, such as an interesting tree. Once you have gradually cleared away unwanted plants and weeds, you will then have a better idea of the overall design.

TIPS WHEN CLEARING YOUR SITE

● The benefit of a neglected garden is that the soil is often very good indeed, containing much organic matter provided by years of rotting leaves. Heavy clay soil will be much improved by this humus. Shredded leaves and branches can be composted to make a humus. Remember to let it decompose sufficiently before it's used on the garden.

● Take care when clearing out a neglected pond not to damage the liner, as it may be perfectly all right and could last for many more years. If trees have grown large near an old pond, it may be wise to move the pond elsewhere to a more open site.

● Overgrown or neglected gardens are often a haven for wildlife. Frogs, toads and newts are all beneficial to the gardener and so should be released back into the garden once the work has finished.

● Once trees and large shrubs have been pruned, see what reappears at ground level, as certain bulbs and plants lie dormant until light encourages them into a new lease of life.

PRUNING

WHY WE PRUNE

Many garden shrubs are quite happy if left unpruned, but, some of our favourites, if left unchecked, can grow into quite enormous specimens. I've seen the trusty mock orange, for instance, reaching twenty feet into the sky where the benefit of the deliciously scented flowers was wasted and nothing could grow in the shade underneath it.

Generally, we all overplant our gardens, because we want instant results. Usually, the plants look fine for a couple of years, but then some begin to take over, and you have to decide which to take out, or whether to keep pruning them. Overplanted schemes can work admirably if they are kept in check, but often the natural shape of the plant is lost due to constant trimming.

Hard pruning in spring, however, can result in a burst of growth that in a couple of months will look lush and natural. You end up with a much more 'fluid' bush, not one that has grown dense and rigid as a result of light, regular clipping. Some trees and shrubs, especially evergreens, however, will never return to their former glory once they have been left to grow out of control and then are cut back hard.

DEALING WITH PERENNIAL WEEDS

● If you don't mind using weedkillers, then use one containing glyphosate, which if used sensibly, and allowed to dry on the foliage, should not be harmful to pets. This chemical takes three to four weeks to show its effects on the weeds, as it takes time to work its way to the roots. So don't cut foliage down until it has died off. Only use in the growing season and avoid making any contact with plants or shrubs you want to keep.

● If you do not wish to use chemicals, you will have to dig the weeds out manually. Any root sections of perennial weeds left in the ground may grow again in spring and will prove to be a headache later on.

● See also Chapter 5, page 67.

Clipped, neat hedges and topiary, work very effectively in formal gardens and schemes, and although a clipped specimen can 'hold together' an otherwise disorganized border, I generally like to keep the two themes separate.

Pruning regularly enables you to grow many more plants than nature intended. By thinning-out shrubs and trees, a lower level planting of perennials or low shrubs can be achieved, which otherwise would not grow in the deep shade. These plants not only give extra colour to borders, but also keep weeds down and provide a safe haven for wildlife.

HOW TO PRUNE

Always seek professional help if you're unconfident about tackling pruning yourself. If you do want to try and prune some of the trees and shrubs, always use sharp tools, otherwise infection will creep into damaged cuts and cause rotting or disease. Be particularly careful with these sharp tools and especially so with chainsaws. These can be very dangerous in inexperienced hands. It may be best to call in professional tree surgeons if your particular tree is very high.

If you are patient, it's far better to prune certain species of overgrown shrubs and trees gradually over two to three years, bringing down the height a little more each year. This is especially important if it is a rare or valuable plant.

Always make the pruning cuts just above a bud and preferably sloping downwards from it. Also, always prune to an outward-facing bud on shrubs, as this is the direction the new shoot will grow, producing a desirable shape.

Suckers may appear at the base of hard-pruned shrubs and trees, so make sure these are quickly removed as far down as possible.

Pruning cuts have been traditionally painted with a black tar-like substance to protect the wound from infection. However, long and thorough research has indicated that wounds may be best left with nothing at all painted onto them.

Once large overgrown trees and shrubs have been pruned to allow in more light, existing smaller plants will soon return to their former glory.

PRUNING TREES

With most trees, the idea is to create a goblet-shaped crown to let in light and air and to make the tree look well balanced. This rule does not apply to all trees (see below).

Generally, pruning is best carried out in the dormant period, between October and March, but summer pruning can be useful to reduce vigour (often used when pruning apple trees in July). There are, surprisingly, many trees that can be pruned all year round, such as lime, London plane, sycamore and oak.

There are some trees that go against these general rules:

- *Columnar trees.* These naturally grow in an erect, upright fashion. Remove any stray branches that grow out past the main shape. They are good for confined spaces. Examples include *Crataegus monogyna* 'Stricta' (upright hawthorn), *Fagus sylvatica* 'Dawyck' (columnar beech), *Prunus* 'Amanogawa' (pillar cherry).
- *Weeping trees.* These need very little pruning. If any rogue, upright shoots appear from the main trunk, or any branches grow at odd angles to the rest, prune out cleanly to keep an even, balanced shape. They are good for small gardens, or as a focal point. Examples include *Betula pendula* 'Youngii' (weeping birch), *Malus* 'Red Jade' (weeping crab apple), *Pyrus salicifolia* 'Pendula' (weeping silver-leaved pear).
- *Pollarded trees.* Branches are cut back close to the main trunk every few years to encourage fresh growth. Examples include

Tilia (lime), *Salix alba* (bat willow), Robinia (green false acacia).
- *Pleached trees.* Branches are trained across wires. Tilia is usually used for this group. Seen often in French market squares.

PRUNING FRUIT TREES

Yearly pruning is not essential and can be detrimental if flowering shoots are cut off, and hence the fruit. The general idea is to produce an open crown allowing in light and air, which assists in flower and fruit production.

- *Apples.* Prune in the dormant period, if necessary, by keeping centre open and removing crossing-over or diseased wood. Shoots that are growing too tall should be reduced also. In summer, a second pruning may be useful. Reducing sideshoots back to a few buds (spurs) at this time of year, discourages growth, but encourages flower-bud production. Summer pruning may be useful if you are trying to slow down particularly vigorous varieties.
- *Cherries and plums.* These are best pruned in mid-summer when the wounds will heal quickly, thus preventing silver-leaf disease entering. Regular pruning is not required.
- *Pears.* Try to create an open framework and fruit-producing spurs (as for apple). Regular pruning is not required.

Fruit trees can also be trained as cordons and espaliers but a neglected tree could be difficult to reinstate in this form.

PRUNING SHRUBS

Evergreens

Most evergreens will not need regular pruning. If you want to keep them orderly, trim them through the summer. Only prune lightly after flowering if really necessary. More severe pruning is best tackled in spring. Some evergreens, once a certain size, will not reshoot when pruned hard, and may have to be replaced (e.g. cistus).

If you are severely pruning variegated shrubs, watch out for all-green shoots that may appear in spring which will soon take over from the variegated part unless pruned out early.

Conifers can be trimmed in summer with hedge-trimmers; if you do this in winter, the newly revealed inner shoots are exposed to the cold and wind and this causes browning off.

I like to use secateurs if possible when pruning individual conifers; hedge-trimmers cause very dense regrowth but thinning the outside shoots with secateurs allows air to circulate and they look more natural when pruned in this way. This is certainly important if you are pruning spreading junipers, as you will want to maintain that irregular look.

Never cut conifers too hard back. They rarely regrow from old, leafless wood. Only yew and some thujas will regrow successfully.

Pruning advice on some common evergreens:

- *Aucuba japonica* 'Variegata' (spotted laurel). Only prune if you want to restrict growth; best to use secateurs in spring, to cut individual stems off, rather than shear through leaves which will turn brown.

- Berberis (barberry). Small-leaved varieties do not need regular pruning; can be pruned with electric shears or secateurs; prune after flowering in early summer, but you may not have any berries that year.
- *Buxus* (box). Pinch out extended growth in summer or use shears if a hedge.
- Ceanothus (Californian lilac). This wall-shrub is best pruned with secateurs just after flowering in spring/summer to train it flat on the wall or fence; prune late-flowering varieties in mid-spring.
- Choisya (Mexican orange blossom). I prune mine (yellow and green versions) lightly in mid-summer to keep them a reasonable size; new growth is then produced before autumn.
- Cistus (rock rose). Generally leave alone, unless they get too large; prune lightly in mid-summer after flowering with secateurs, to keep in order.
- Cotoneaster. Prune any time really, but best prune back extended growth in late summer to reveal the berries for winter display (as in pyracantha). Prune in spring if foliage is more important.
- Cytisus (broom). These often die if pruned in winter; best time is just after flowering, usually in early summer.
- Elaeagnus. Prune out any 'all-green' shoots emerging from variegated plants. To keep in order, prune in mid- to late spring.
- Escallonia. You can use shears on small-leaved varieties, otherwise secateurs; prune if needed after flowering in mid-summer.
- Hebe. Use secateurs to tidy up in mid-spring; cut leggy specimens quite hard back, but not into leafless old wood.

ABOVE *Maintaining a slightly overgrown feel can add character and mystery to a garden.*

● *Ilex* (holly). Best pruned in April if needed; can be trained into various shapes, by selective pruning in summer.
● *Lonicera nitida*. Can be pruned any time throughout the summer; shears are fine.
● Mahonia. If you need to, prune in mid-spring after flowering.

OPPOSITE *The gardens at Heligan in Cornwall were left untouched for decades before renovation.*

● *Prunus laurocerasus* (laurel). Prune as hard as you like in April. In fact, they're pretty hard to kill even if you prune in the dead of winter!
● Pyracantha. If it is growing on a fence or wall, train main shoots until they've reached their desired proportions, keeping the plant as flat as possible, then prune back shoots to expose the beautiful berries in late summer.
● Rhododendrons. These don't generally need pruning, but old, leggy individuals can be cut hard back in March; no flowers will appear for at least two or three years; always try to remove flower trusses when faded, as this will encourage better flowering the following year.

TRANSPLANTING SHRUBS

- Lifting and replanting **evergreens** is best done in early to mid-autumn or early spring. Always keep a large rootball when transplanting evergreens, as they still have to support their foliage through the winter. Protect transplanted evergreens with windbreak netting to help reduce water loss from the foliage. Keep watered well, even through the winter.

- Transplanted **deciduous shrubs** can survive with fewer roots when lifted than evergreens. The top growth can be reduced to balance off the stem-root ratio; this often helps strong regrowth in the spring.

- Pine trees seem to be the only **conifer** that can survive transplanting with a minimum root system. Because of their wind-tolerant needles, they release less moisture and so have time to produce new roots before dehydrating. Christmas tree spray, which helps prevent needle-drop, works well on replanted conifers as it cuts down water loss from the foliage and hence gives the plant time to generate new roots to support itself.

- If replanting mature shrubs, ensure that any damaged roots have been cleanly cut to prevent infection.

- Stake replanted shrubs to prevent any movement in winter which allows water to collect around the trunk and increases the risk of root rot.

Deciduous shrubs

A simple pruning tip is to prune winter/spring-flowering shrubs such as forsythia and *Jasminum nudiflorum* after flowering, and mid- to late summer-flowering shrubs, such as buddleia and lavatera, in spring (although you may wish to tidy these up a bit in winter); in this way you will not lose the flowers by pruning off the flower buds.

Pruning advice on some deciduous shrubs is given below.

- *Buddleia davidii* (butterfly bush). Best reduced by half in mid-autumn to reduce rocking, then pruned down to 60 cm (2 ft) in early spring.

- *Buddleia alternifolia*. This goes against the norm as it flowers on last year's wood in early summer; if necessary, thin out just after flowering in mid-summer.

- Cornus (dogwood). If you want the red or yellow stems to look their best in winter, then prune hard in early spring, down to 30 cm (1 ft) from the ground; if you prefer a more graceful large shrub with white flowers and white berries, then leave alone or just trim lightly.

- Deutzia. To keep in check, prune just after flowering in mid-summer; remove old shoots to thin out bush and reduce rest by one third.

- Forsythia. If left alone, forsythia will grow enormous unless you choose one of the new dwarf varieties; best pruned half-way down just after flowering in late spring and thin out old wood.

- Hydrangea. Mop-head hydrangeas don't need too much pruning; if you cut them hard they may not flower for two years; best to remove old flower heads in spring and perhaps thin out weak shoots.

- *Hydrangea paniculata*. These flower on new growth from the same year so can be pruned hard in spring.
- *Hypericum* 'Hidcote'. You can be quite ruthless by pruning hard over winter or spring, to keep orderly.
- Lavatera (mallow). Prune by one third in mid-autumn to reduce wind rock and to tidy up, then by another third in spring.
- Philadelphus (mock orange). These vigorous shrubs are best thinned out and then pruned just after flowering in mid-summer; smaller growing varieties are now available for small gardens and don't need regular pruning.
- Ribes (flowering currant). Prune just after flowering in early summer, if needed; thin out and reduce shoots by half to form a neat bush.
- Roses: hybrid teas. Prune by about one third in autumn, then by another third in early spring, as much as 5–6 buds from the ground.
- Floribunda. Prune lightly and thin out in autumn, then by half in early spring.
- Shrub (old-fashioned). These don't generally need a harsh pruning regime: thin out when the 'hips' have gone in winter/ spring. Reduce by one third in early spring (remember the harder you prune, the more vigorous the plant will grow).
- Spiraea. There are so many different species of this very useful bush; late-flowering types such as *S. japonica* 'Anthony Waterer', *S. aitchisonii* (now *Sorbaria aitchisonii*), *S. japonica* 'Gold Flame', *S.j.* 'Little Princess', should be pruned almost to a stump in later winter/early spring; earlier ones such as *S.* 'Arguta', *S.* × *vanhouttei*, *S. nipponica* 'Snowmound' are best pruned just after flowering.

- Weigela. Does not need much pruning until it becomes leggy or too large. Cut back hard in early spring if the attractive foliage is what you prefer; for the best flowering display, either leave alone or prune after flowering in mid-summer.

DIVISION OF PERENNIALS

Many perennials appreciate being divided in their dormant period and transplanted, especially if they have remained untouched for years.

Even perennials that have reached mammoth proportions, can be lifted at the right time of the year and divided up to produce new plants; these can be replanted and any excess swapped with neighbours or friends.

Dividing perennials is best done in autumn or early spring. After digging up the clump, use two forks back-to-back and lever these against each other to pull the clump apart. Some perennials don't mind being chopped in half with a sharp spade or cut with a large knife.

The Overgrown Garden

Robert was in a real dilemma: the longer he left his garden the worse it was getting, but he hadn't a clue where to start! Bindweed and brambles had smothered most of the plants and shrubs in the garden. A pussy willow's spreading, twisted branches were stretching out over at least half of the garden. It had blown over a few years previously and, propped up by the fence, had rerooted; it now had a real tortured, but potentially interesting look, a possible focal point. There was also an overgrown apple tree in the undergrowth that had obviously not been touched for years.

It was very difficult to see what style the garden had been originally, if indeed it had ever been designed or planned at all. There were a couple of paving stones visible in a gap through the weeds indicating a possible path or patio hidden from view.

Design

Both Robert and I agreed that a slightly wild look with a natural feel would be the most favourable design, rather than anything too suburban and ordinary.

The willow, on closer inspection, had developed a really weird branch formation: this would be a 'plus point' for our design, as it could, with careful pruning give a real 'jungle book' effect.

The apple tree would become a corner focal point after pruning and the planting would be generally natural and unfussy.

The retaining rock wall at the front would be fine once cleared of weeds; plants such as alpines could be planted to hold it together and give some colour.

LEFT *Even an impenetrable jungle is tameable!*

OPPOSITE *By careful pruning, a semi-wild garden can be maintained and enjoyed.*

Materials

furniture (wooden table and chairs set,
treated with preservative)
logs for seat
ornamental oak stump
pruning equipment: chainsaw, loppers and
secateurs

Step-by-step

1 **Assessing the situation and clearing
the site** The only things worth keeping
after close inspection were the apple, a leggy
pear, a wild elderberry (as it would be good for
the birds), a couple of wild roses for their
attractive hips and the over-hanging willow. A
carpet of wild ivy grew in patches under the
trees which we decided to keep as a sort of
lawn substitute. A wild blackberry was
replanted against the fence as it had the most
delicious fruits.

As Robert didn't want to use chemicals, we
dug the perennial weeds out by hand.

While clearing, we discovered under the leaf
mould about two dozen Victorian edging tiles
and an area of old council slabs, which we
immediately put aside for reuse.

2 **Pruning** We decided to leave the
elderberry as it was heavily laden with
fruit and not only ornamental but obviously a
natural larder for wildlife. I thinned out the
crown of the apple tree and cut out any
crossing-over branches. Then the upright

shoots were cut down by one third to
encourage fruiting buds.

The pear was so weak and spindly it would
normally have been taken out, but it had been
struggling for so long under the willow and
apple branches, I decided to give it a chance,
now more light was being let in.

The pussy willow was monstrous but we all
loved it. The roots and main trunk were in the
neighbour's garden, but Robert still had the
benefit of those wonderful theatrical branches.
Because there was far too much weight on one
side, which could cause it to fall over once and
for all, we used delicate chainsaw work to
remove unwanted branches. We kept a couple
of branches hanging across the garden to keep a
sense of adventure when walking through it.
Many side shoots were removed to let more light
onto the plants below until it looked just right.

3 **Seating areas and stepping stones**
Where an old patio might have been, we
relevelled the grubby paving and edged it with
the Victorian-style edging tiles we had
discovered earlier. To one side of this new area
we created a log seat, made from 2 chunky log
sections 90 × 15 cm (3 ft × 6 in) as legs, buried
30 cm (12 in) into the ground. Two sections of
a split log formed the seat. Not the most
comfortable place in the world to sit but it
looked just right!

Another small seating area was made in the
corner under the trees as a shady refuge in
summer.

Stepping stones of more old slabs were
positioned to lead from the house to the two
sitting areas.

A rustic log seat made from recycled tree trunks.

4 **Plants and decoration** The plants we used were hardy, easy-to-grow, natural-looking species. Some nearer the house were in more sun, but others further back had to tolerate more of a shady environment (see chapter The Shady Garden). Most will require no regular maintenance but were watered well for the first couple of months.

A mass of colour wasn't important for our wild-looking scene. We used groups of violas in natural swathes, to create the effect of bluebells in early summer.

Large rhododendrons were planted in the semi-shade of the apple to give bulk, and beautiful flowers in spring and early summer. Graceful cotoneasters were chosen for their bright red berries giving colour and food for birds in autumn/winter.

A beautiful ancient root of an oak tree was used as decoration on the side of the seating area which seemed far more impressive than any man-made focal point!

5 **Furniture** A simple wooden table and chairs were chosen. These were inexpensive, but fitted in perfectly with the semi-wild garden we had forged out of the undergrowth and complemented the rustic log seat.

PLANTS USED FOR THE TV GARDEN

- 3 × ground-cover 'County' roses (see page 74).
- 3 × *Cotoneaster salicifolius floccosus*. White flowers and red berries in autumn/winter; evergreen, arching habit.
- 1 × *Cotoneaster* 'Rothschildianus'. White flowers followed by yellow berries in autumn/winter; evergreen, arching habit.
- 3 × *Spiraea japonica* 'Gold Mound'. Bushy habit; bright golden-yellow leaves; pink flowers.
- 3 × caryopteris (see page 28).
- 3 × *Rubus calycinoïdes* (see page 74).
- 1 × rhododendron hybrid 'Christmas Cheer' (see page 43).
- 1 × rhododendron hybrid 'Wilgen's Ruby'. Huge, ruby-red flowers in early summer; large growing.
- 50 × mixed alpines for bank (see chapter The Rock Garden).
- 7 trays of bedding violas (see page 25).

chapter seven

The Family Garden

There is no greater challenge than mixing children and gardening harmoniously!

When I was a toddler, apparently I was only interested in finding any frog, toad, spider, worm or insect that I possibly could. This meant delving into my mother's prize patio or garden plants (usually at their peak of flowering) to find them. When I was older, scoring a goal was far more important than worrying about knocking flat any plants that may have been planted there!

A family garden should be enjoyed by everyone, adults as well as children and the design should endeavour to cater for all needs.

DESIGN

There are many aspects of a family garden to be considered. Adults may need some seclusion so a big concern is to create separate areas where adults can relax and children can have fun and learn at the same time. Equally there are several dangers to avoid, particularly if there are toddlers around. The box on page 96 lists these.

CHILDREN'S PLAY AREA

If you build a specific area for the children to play in, it can be disguised by careful use of trellis work, or island beds of shrubs which, as they grow, will hide the view of the swings, etc., behind them.

Level areas for games should always be part of the design, leaving enough room on the lawn for ball games, if you have space. It is important to use robust shrubs and plants around any play area that won't mind the weight of a falling child and may indeed cushion the fall.

Sandpits

If you haven't got any pets that might care to use the sandpit as a litter tray, sandpits are fun for small children.

Always use silver sand for sandpits, as it does not stain clothing, and cover them when not in use to keep the rain and cats out.

A family garden should be fun for everyone.

Climbing frame and lawn areas

Fun and aesthetically pleasing climbing frames and games can be spread throughout the garden if you don't want a specific area so there's a sense of adventure. However, if you do make a play area, use 'play bark' under swings and frames, at least 15 cm (6 in) thick for safety. Non-slip slabs should be used for access paths.

If you have a lawn that the children can play on, use ryegrass which is far more tolerant of wear and tear.

CHILDREN'S GARDENS

It is often a good idea to set aside an area specifically intended as the children's own little garden; this cultivates an interest in gardening from a young age.

Quick-growing plants are usually fascinating to youngsters. Choose plants such as nasturtiums, courgettes and sunflowers for quick, fun results. Mustard and cress can be grown on a window sill, on damp tissue.

Build their own little raised vegetable garden out of 15 cm (6 in) high gravel boards, or sleepers; new soil can be introduced which will be easier to work and will warm up more quickly in spring. A cold frame can be made out of a wooden frame and sheets of clear Perspex.

Mini-tools are available at most garden centres which the children will love.

TAKE CARE!

● Some plants and particularly berries are poisonous. Check existing plants and do not introduce new ones that are dangerous.

● Sharp or prickly plants can also cause injury. Even harmless-looking things like pampas grass can cut a child's hand if pulled along its length.

● Ponds, even shallow ones, are particularly dangerous for toddlers. Make them very safe, or fill them in as a sandpit until they're older.

● Awkward steps are easy to trip on and it's always best to make these more obvious with a line of darker bricks or slabs.

● Gravel is a problem surface in a family garden – children love to throw it about and it is a difficult surface to ride a bike on.

● Dog and cat mess can cause illness (even blindness) so always clear it up immediately. Sandpits and gravel are favourite spots for pets!

● Climbing frames must never be built on a hard surface, nor rough timber used as it may result in splinters.

● It is best not to use chemicals in the garden if children are present, even though most are allegedly safe. Keep all fertilizers and chemicals in a locked cupboard.

● Carelessly left tools can be dangerous; always store them in a safe place.

● Bamboo canes stuck in the ground are a potential hazard to eyes. Protective rubber caps are available to put on the cane ends.

PONDS

If the children are older, then they may 'demand' a pond for fish, or wildlife. I would always advise building one near the house, for various reasons.

1   For safety reasons it's far better for parents to be able to see what's going on from the house.
2   In winter the children can see what's happening in their pond without trekking through the garden (muddy feet!).
3   Everyone else can appreciate the pond and its inhabitants far more often than if it's some distance away (a general rule of mine when positioning a pond).

An existing pond, or indeed a new one, will need fencing off in some way, if younger children are around. This can look ugly, unless designed very cleverly.

Frogspawn is always fascinating to young children and if it is introduced to your pond, the adult frogs should return to spawn there themselves in a couple of years. Introduce your children to frogs, toads and newts and they will learn early on to appreciate wildlife.

WILDLIFE

Youngsters should be encouraged to take an interest in nature. Most garden creatures are beneficial, so teach the children that they are our friends. Later on in this chapter there is a list of wildlife (page 100) they may encounter and a section on bird boxes (page 100).

PLANTINGS WITH CHILDREN IN MIND

It is pointless designing fancy schemes which may be spoilt. Choose easy plants for children to grow and robust more mature plants near play areas.

SEEDS

Annual plants grown from seed are normally quick to germinate and grow. Some of the best vegetables for children are:

- mustard and cress
- lettuces
- carrots
- radishes
- runner beans
- courgettes
- pumpkins
- tomatoes

These vegetables are best started in small pots on the window sill and planted in their own little vegetable garden in late spring to early summer.

Annual flowers that are always good fun are:

- nasturtiums
- sunflowers
- helichrysum
- cosmos
- larkspur
- clarkia.

These hardy annuals can be sown shallowly, directly into the ground in early spring and should be marked with sticks or lines of sand, so the children can tell where they are and not to pull them out thinking they're weeds later.

Mimosa pudica (sensitive plant) is a fun indoor plant, as the leaves and stems close and droop when touched. Also, the Venus flytrap is a fascinating, carnivorous plant which children love.

SHRUBS

One of my first memories of gardening was planting a buddleia with my father and marvelling at the multitude of beautiful butterflies that it later attracted with its flowers.

Berried shrubs are great for attracting birds into the garden; they eat the fruit, then 'pass' the seed which is usually the poisonous part of the berry. This is how the seedlings spread to other areas, thus ensuring its survival. The human digestive system, however, is far stronger than the bird's, and so will break down the seed's protective shell, releasing its poison. This is why yew, for instance, is eaten readily by birds, but is deadly to cattle and humans.

Most shrub berries are not harmful, but merely taste pretty awful, so children are not tempted to eat them more than once! Some, however, are poisonous and must be avoided (see page 101). To be totally safe, berried plants are best avoided altogether if you have young children, or if they often come to visit you.

Here are some non-poisonous chunky, robust shrubs that won't be too offended if a child happens to fall on them. They are fairly pliable and shouldn't be damaged easily.

Sandpits should be designed so that they can be converted into a pool or bed when the children are older. Always use silver sand.

ROBUST SHRUBS

- buddleia (butterfly bush)
- *Buxus* (box)
- bamboo (should be warned about stiff, upright new growth in summer)
- cornus (dogwood)
- choisya (Mexican orange blossom)
- *Ceanothus* 'Gloire de Versailles' (deciduous Californian lilac)
- deutzia
- escallonia
- cotinus (smoke bush)
- cytisus (broom)
- forsythia
- griselina
- heathers
- *Hebe salicifolia*
- *Hebe* 'Marjorie'
- *Kerria japonica*
- lavatera (mallow)
- *Lonicera pileata*
- *Lonicera nitida* 'Baggesons Gold'
- osmanthus
- photinia (red robin)
- pittosporum
- potentilla
- *Prunus laurocerasus* 'Zabeliana'
- *Prunus lusitanica*
- ribes (flowering currant)
- senecio
- spiraea (most varieties)
- tamarix
- weigela.

Sunflowers are certainly one of the most rewarding plants for the young gardener.

CONIFERS

Many 'fir trees' have soft, pliable foliage that will bend and absorb a child's weight. They are also thick and evergreen and therefore useful to screen off unsightly objects. Birds will love to nest in them too.

Conifers are best grown in a light situation, and not in a waterlogged soil.

WILDLIFE IN THE GARDEN

If you create the right environment, there are many creatures which will be attracted to your garden. The children will enjoy learning about them.

Hedgehogs and birds are common visitors and if you have a pond amphibians may make their home nearby in and around it. There are also several reptiles which may visit, which are dry and smooth, contrary to people's expectations. Here is a list of possible garden visitors:

SNAKES AND LIZARDS

- *Grass snake.* Olive or light green, with black and yellow on the side of the head, reaching 1.2 m (4 ft); harmless and shy.
- *Adder.* Poisonous but very shy; handsome dark zigzags over greyish body. Not aggressive unless handled.
- *Common lizard.* About 10 cm (4 in) long and sadly not that common; prefers heather areas with sandy soil.
- *Sand lizard.* Unfortunately now very rare. Attractive reptile, which you would be privileged but unlikely to have in your garden.

FROGS, TOADS AND NEWTS

- *Common frog.* A great friend to man as it feeds on garden pests; needs water to breed, but feeds on land, mainly at night.
- *Edible frog.* Introduced from France many years ago; has a characteristic yellow stripe down its back; lives mainly in water. Uncommon.
- *Marsh frog.* Introduced from Europe. Much bigger than the other two species. Croaks very loudly in spring. Uncommon.

- *Common toad.* My favourite garden animal; tough, leathery skin, preferring to walk rather than hop; spawn is long and tubular, laid amongst pond weed.
- *Natterjack toad.* Very rare; lives in sandy areas; smaller than common toad, with a light creamy-yellow stripe down its back.
- *Common newt.* Lives much of the year in ponds, but is also found under things in the garden; can be kept for a short while in an aquarium, so it can be seen under water; eats small worms and insects in the water.
- *Palmate newt.* Quite rare; slightly smaller than the common newt, still with distinctive orange underside; browny colour above.
- *Crested newt.* Largest of the newts, reaching 15 cm (6 in) long; black above and bright yellow underneath.

BIRD BOXES FOR THE GARDEN

What a great feeling it is to see a bird carrying nesting materials into a box you've put up. Your children will be equally fascinated, especially if they have helped build it. Blue tits and robins will tolerate the odd peek into the viewing hole!

Remember to position the box with the hole facing east, as otherwise they'll often ignore it. Also remember not to feed the birds in summer when there should be enough food in the garden; particularly do not feed nuts then, as these can choke young chicks.

Blue tits need a box with a hole of 2–2.5 cm (¾–1 in). Robins will nest in anything from an old kettle to a discarded boot, but they will often nest in a box with one third open-fronted.

PLANTS TO AVOID WITH YOUNG CHILDREN

Toxic if eaten

- aconitum (winter aconites)
- colchicum (autumn crocus)
- *Convallaria majalis* (lily-of-the-valley)
- daphne
- datura
- digitalis (foxglove)
- pernettya
- *Gloriosa superba* (climbing lily)
- hyoscyamus
- laburnum
- lantana
- *Nerium oleander* (oleander)
- phytolacca
- *Ricinus communis*
- *Solanum dulcamara* (deadly nightshade group)
- taxus (yew)
- veratrum

- euonymus
- gaultheria
- helleborus
- *Hypericum perforatum*
- ipomoea (morning glory)
- iris
- *Juniperus sabina*
- kalmia (calico bush)
- ligustrum (privet)
- lupinus
- ornithogalum (snowdrops)
- polygonatum
- *Primula obconica* (indoor primula)
- *Prunus laurocerasus* (laurel)
- rhamnus
- ruta (rue)
- scilla
- thuja

Plants that may cause sickness or irritation if eaten

- arum
- dieffenbachia (indoor plant)
- aesculus (horse chestnut family)
- agrostemma
- aquilegia
- brugmansia
- caltha (marsh marigold)
- catharanthus
- delphinium

Plants that may cause skin allergy/ irritation

- alstroemeria
- echium
- euphorbia
- ficus (rubber plant)
- fremontodendron (Californian glory)
- × *Cupressocyparis leylandii* (Leylandii conifers)
- narcissus (daffodils)
- schefflera (indoor plant)
- tulips

The Family Garden

Rosie and her three children had inherited a patch of dead grass and a deluge of prickly weeds as their garden. One side was dominated by a high concrete wall, the other had a high wooden fence. The overall area was only about 15 × 5 m (48 × 16 ft) so careful use of the minimal space was essential. There was also a rickety, old swing.

Rosie had attempted to plant the odd shrub, but her boisterous kids soon put paid to her efforts!

A very narrow plot needs extra thought when designing.

Materials

16 × 45 × 45 cm (1½ × 1½ ft) light grey paving slabs
2 bags cement
10 bags sand
blackboard paint
wood preservative
4 × posts 1.8 m × 10 cm × 10 cm (6 ft × 4 in × 4 in)
4 Metposts
4 × 10 × 5 cm (4 × 2 in) timbers (horizontals)
10 × beams 2 m × 10 cm × 5 cm (6 ft × 4 in × 2 in) ('roof' sections)
swing and rope
sandpit and silver sand

As a musician and mother Rosie had always wanted a garden both as a secluded place to play her harp and for the children to play and have fun in. They all wanted colourful plants to look after.

Design

Many things had to be considered here, as a modest space such as this needed very careful thought. Somehow, a secluded area had to be created so that Rosie could have a sense of her own space. The children needed a play area in the garden and small beds they could call their own.

OPPOSITE *A family garden can be fun, practical and attractive.*

The far corner seemed the best place to use as Rosie's area: an L-shaped pergola would really add to the feeling of privacy. The shape matched in perfectly with narrowness of the plot and would, in fact, make the garden appear larger than it was. It would be a perfect support for new climbers and the large clematis that was growing on the wall behind.

With limited space it was good to give a double use to this area, so part of the pergola design included a space for the swing to be attached.

The concrete wall was so dismal we decided to paint it with wood preservative to make the colour more natural. The kids wanted somewhere they would be allowed to use chalks, so we decided to paint a section of the wall with blackboard paint.

Outdoor chessboards are very strong and dramatic and I included this idea in the design using black and white paving (the black being painted onto light grey slabs). This mini-patio could also be used for various other outdoor games.

A sandpit is an essential part of any garden for young children. We discussed making one ourselves, but the kids had seen one they loved, in the shape of a giant purple and yellow bug.

Step-by-step

1 **Clearing the site** Firstly, everything in the garden, including all the play gear, was removed, children and all. The remaining grass and weeds were dug out using spades to remove the roots, firstly strimming the growth down to ground level to make it easier.

2 **Painting the wall and blackboard** The girls painted the concrete wall using fencing preservative. A large space was left for the blackboard; the blackboard paint dried within one hour, but was not used until the end of the day!

3 **The pergola** The wood we used was chunky, pressure-treated timber, used normally as fence posts. Metposts were knocked onto the posts first, then the post and Metpost knocked in together. These metal spikes save using concrete to keep the post in place and speed up the process. They also prevent the posts rotting.

Once the uprights were in place (about 1.2 m (4 ft) apart and 1.5 m (5 ft) from the wall), the cross-supports (horizontals) were nailed to them at a height of about 2 m (6 ft) from the ground. These timbers were used to support the 'roof' sections by nailing them 60 cm (2 ft) apart and at a slight upward angle to be fixed onto the wall/fence. The angle was created for no other reason than it looked far better than horizontal.

The swing was fixed to sturdy hooks that were screwed to the cross-beams which were strong enough to take even my weight!

Chunky bark chips were brought in as a soft and attractive surface under the pergola, a pleasant floor for Rosie's harp-playing and a good material for the children to play on.

4 **The paving** An area about 2 × 2 m (6 × 6 ft) was marked out, and 10 cm (4 in) of the soil dug out. This enabled a thick bed of sand and cement to be filled in before

A simple L-shaped pergola can have many uses.

as main features, with the lower level filled with celosia, which have a weird brain-like flower that Rosie and the children were fascinated with.

Two large, beautifully planted hanging baskets looked dazzling on the pergola and stems of the existing *Clematis montana* were tied onto the top rails which would cover the top completely in time.

6 **The lawn** Fresh topsoil was barrowed in to cover the old ground to a depth of 2–4 cm (½–1½ in). The soil was raked level, and fresh ryegrass turves laid, which are very hard-wearing.

Rosie was reminded to water it every day in dry sunny weather for a couple of weeks, until it had all rooted into the new soil and started to grow. It could be cut in four weeks.

The very final touch was positioning the sandpit and filling it with silver sand.

the paving was laid. It needed to be solid as there was obviously going to be a lot of activity on the area.

Alternate slabs were painted again with blackboard paint to give a checkerboard effect.

5 **The beds** By standing back and seeing how things were shaping up, I could visualize where the beds should go. We decided to plant three mature ligustrum (golden privet) and a large, red weigela which all gave an instant feeling of maturity. We told the children that privet leaves will make you feel sick if eaten.

Under the shrubs we planted annual rudbeckia and other colourful bedding plants which the kids really appreciated.

The final bed was created beyond the black and white patio: this had two large phormiums

PLANTS USED FOR THE TV GARDEN

- 3 × *Ligustrum ovalifolium* 'Aureum'
- 1 × *Weigela* 'Bristol Ruby'
- 24 × celosia
- 50 × *Rudbeckia* 'Marmalade'
- 2 × *Phormium tenax* 'Variegatum'
- 24 × mini chrysanthemums (see page 79)
- 42 sq m (50 sq yds) meadow turf (ryegrass)
- 2 hanging baskets containing 'Surfina' petunias, felicia, helichrysum and dwarf Marguerites

chapter eight

The Roof Garden

If you are lucky enough to have a flat roof area, you may have underestimated the huge potential available to create a wonderful garden space. Many people wonder what on earth can be grown at such a great height, what lightweight materials are available and how to irrigate the garden. All these problems can be solved and will be covered in this chapter.

Roof gardens are generally created for people who have not the ground space available for a more traditional garden. A roof can be transformed into a tranquil area that brings nature closer and takes the owners far away from the hustle and bustle of city life.

I've seen beautiful, lush gardens on office block roofs, used by the overstressed staff to recharge their batteries at lunchtime. I have even known of a garden that has been created on a garage roof, for a gentleman to escape from his overactive and noisy children. So, there are many

Even the smallest area can be utilized to form an extra room outside without enormous cost.

advantages to having a roof-top garden. They are wonderful places to entertain friends and should be an asset to your property.

Before you get too excited, the tedious part must be dealt with first.

No excess weight should ever be placed on a roof area without prior consultation with a structural engineer. Plans of the building need to be examined closely so that a clear calculation can be made of exactly how much weight can be placed on your potential roof garden.

DESIGN

Sometimes merely a place to lounge on a deck-chair is all that is required, but for the more ambitious and imaginative, any theme or style is possible.

Practical needs must be carefully considered, especially if you have young children. Gravel, for instance, is favoured by kids to kick and throw around, which is bad news above a busy street in the city. Floor coverings are described later; there are many options available (see page 109–10).

A design including a mass of plants will require a lot of attention in the summer and will reduce the space available for games etc., so careful thought must be paid to who will actually use the garden. When designing a garden on a roof, always adapt the theme to suit the person or people using it, to give the maximum long-term pleasure.

Drawing a plan will be especially useful here, as a relatively small area requires best use of space.

Here are a few important things to consider.

• The main, obvious limiting factor is stress. Most roofs are not designed to hold excessive weight and, therefore, must be strengthened accordingly before any attempts are made to create a roof garden. This really is highly involved work and will certainly be very expensive.

• Safety is very important, especially if young children are allowed access to your roof. Even merry party-goers may find a quick route to the ground floor unless safety is seriously considered. (See under Boundaries, page 108–9.)

• Working on a flat roof area may cause damage to the waterproof surface. Extra care must be taken to ensure that no sharp items are carelessly placed on the roof and that heavy objects are delicately positioned. Using old carpet or insulation felt under these items will help protect the surface.

• Care must be taken not to block any drainage holes or gullies. Try not to allow excessive amounts of soil or dirt through them as blocked pipes may result.

• Plant choice is crucial to successful high-rise gardening. There is no point subjecting a delicate-leaved maple, for instance, to a very windy, sun-baked site, where its beautiful foliage will get scorched and it will continually dry out. It's far better to choose plants that will naturally thrive in those conditions, such as dwarf pines, Mediterranean plants, etc. (See plantings section on page 114 and 116–19.)

BOUNDARIES

The first thing to tackle when you have decided to take the plunge (not literally, of course!), is the boundary. Often there may be nothing much to divide the roof from the surrounding sky so careful thought must be paid to this.

Never use a solid barrier, such as fencing panels, as a boundary. They do not filter the wind, and could be ripped away in strong gales.

RAILINGS

Metal railings are sometimes present, but may be too stark or too low for your taste. Remember that closing yourself in too much may take away a beautiful view across the city or park. Perhaps you want to shut yourself away, in which case higher railings may be required.

Simply painting rusty or rather dull metal with suitable paint can really liven up otherwise gloomy railings and prolong their life. Growing climbing plants, such as clematis or honeysuckle, through them helps green up the area and give privacy.

Always call a reliable professional to do any dangerous work and to check the safety of your railings, especially if you are fixing any trellis or plants to them.

TRELLISES

With existing railings in place, it is far easier to attach trellis panels to them using thick wire or bolts. This can be cheaper than changing the height of the railings and the wooden trellis gives a more natural look and a better support for climbing plants. If there are no railings it may prove costly to attach suitable posts to your roof before trellises can be fixed.

Bolt-down metal 'sleeves' to hold a post in place are the most practical solution as long as they can be fixed into concrete or another solid surface (check with a structural engineer). These are easily obtainable at garden centres and can be bolted down to the concrete or steel floor. The posts are then slotted into the sleeve-holder ready for the trellis panel.

Expandable trellis is much weaker than the solid type and may not be sufficiently strong to withstand heavy winds. Most solid trellis panels are sold in various heights from 60 cm to 1.8 m (2–6 ft), but only come in 1.8 m (6 ft) lengths, so remember this when positioning the posts!

Plastic windbreak material can be attached to the back of the trellis or railings, to cut down the wind and create a better environment. It may also give more privacy if you are overlooked, without cutting out too much light. It is obtained in rolls and can be secured using plastic-coated wire clematis ties or staples.

HEDGING

Creating a low hedge using conifers or shrubs planted in plastic or wooden troughs can be an easy and relatively inexpensive way to form a boundary to your roof garden. Obviously the safety aspect is hugely increased if this is in front of an existing railing. The filtering effect through the branches cuts down the force of the wind, rather than stopping it dead. (This would cause turbulence on the other side, thus defeating the object.)

In very windy conditions, you may have to bolt the troughs to the deck before they are filled with soil.

Plants suitable for a hedge on your roof are covered in the planting section (see page 118).

FLOOR COVERINGS

GRAVEL

Ornamental gravel is by far the easiest floor covering to apply. Simply pour it on so that there is just enough to cover the surface; too thick a layer makes walking difficult. Note that one 25 kg (56 lb) bag covers about 1 sq m (approx. 10 sq ft).

WOODEN DECKING

This is also easy to lay. I have often laid it simply straight onto the floor without any fixing down, relying on the fact that it fitted tightly into the area. It lasts for years and looks great. If you use them as stepping stones through gravel, it's best to stick them down using bonding cement. The sizes are usually 45 × 45 cm or 60 × 60 cm (18 × 18 in or 24 × 24 in).

WOODEN BOARDS

When fixed to a main framework, boards look fantastic too. This involves more work and has a different look to the decking, giving you long lines instead of many small squares.

Always use pressure-treated timbers which can then be treated with another wood preservative if you prefer a darker shade.

ASTROTURF

This looks like grass but requires no maintenance. It is quite expensive, but if a good-quality one is used, it will last and look good for years. Astroturf needs a very level, even surface, as any bump or unevenness will be very noticeable. It requires a strong glue to fix it firmly to the roof.

IRRIGATION

There is unlikely to be a water supply on your roof and without it gardening becomes impossible. The most effective way is to extend the pipe system to give you a tap on the roof. This will almost certainly involve a professional plumber.

A simple arrangement with pots of flowering plants and shrubs may be all that is needed.

If this is not a feasible option, a large storage water tank can be filled using a hosepipe from the nearest tap. It is then far easier to dip a watering-can in, than to unravel a hose every time.

If you use an attractive container, the water tank could double-up as a fish pool. Fibreglass tanks that have been moulded to look like antique lead are very impressive.

Drip irrigation using a series of pipes from the water supply, although expensive, is a reliable and time-saving way to water your plants. Droplets of water are released steadily which is useful in summer, or an automatic timer can be used to control the flow more accurately.

STYLES AND THEMES

It is often very effective to give a small area a strong theme. Here are a few of my favourites which are particularly suited to roof gardens.

ORIENTAL ROOF GARDEN

A Japanese or oriental-style roof garden has obvious advantages. Its minimalist approach enables you to create the desired effect by merely placing a few choice plants in pots surrounded by gravel.

Plants such as dwarf conifers or bamboos look very effective in this theme. Generally plants originating in these parts of the world are well suited to the conditions up on the roof and life in containers (see page 118–19).

Driftwood and oriental-style ornaments, strategically placed, can really give a strong design theme without great expense.

For my roof garden 'makeover', a Malaysian theme was achieved by using the plants and materials described in this section, plus a very effective artificial pool and a Malaysian hut!

Materials

- *Ornamental pots* Those with oriental symbols or plain ones will do. Glazed pots work well.
- *Gravel* There are many different textures and colours available; it is usually sold in 25 kg (55 lb) bags. Ordinary pea-shingle is by far the cheapest. Buying it loose by the cubic metre is also better value than in bags. If gravel is combined with larger rocks, such as rounded cobbles, an effective picture can be created.
- *Trellis work* Various designs and colours are available. Pressure-treated wood will last well, and can be left untreated for 15–20 years. Painted trellis, on the other hand, may need maintenance. Wood stains such as Sadolin are far better than paint to colour wood.
- *Ornaments* Stone pagodas and lanterns work well. Candles lit up at night are useful when entertaining.
- *Timber structures* Use as focal points to disguise an unsightly view or as a shelter to sit and relax in. (See what I did in the makeover roof garden on page 121.) Note that any structure placed on a windy, exposed site must be securely fixed to the floor.
- *Rock* A few pieces of rock may be enough to achieve the effect, but remember the weight factor. Artificial rock is very useful here, as it is lightweight and easy to handle. A simple method of ageing the artificial rock is described in the Tips section.

Tips

- To 'age' artificial rock, simply brush on sour milk or yoghurt a couple of times a week. After a few weeks, lichens and moss will begin to grow and an 'ancient' piece of rock will take shape.
- Always spray pines and picea with insecticide regularly in spring and mid-summer to prevent red spider and aphid attack.
- Large-growing trees and shrubs can be root and stem pruned to form a bonsai-look relatively quickly and cheaply.
- Look at any 'bargain bay' sections in garden centres. You can often find imperfect shrubs and conifers which are then easily trained to give a bonsai effect.
- Always water azaleas, camellias and rhododendrons regularly, particularly between July and September, as this is when the flower buds are formed for the following spring.
- Remember that very light-coloured gravel may look fine in winter, but in mid-summer, it may be too dazzling.

MEDITERRANEAN ROOF GARDENS

This type of garden is useful if you have a hectic life-style and are likely to leave your plants to look after themselves. Obviously, they do need watering, but these plants can put up with far more neglect than most (see page 119).

The scent of herbs and aromatic plants is a familiar smell in the warmer climates. Most will thrive here perfectly well in a sunny site.

BONSAI

For a true Japanese effect, the art of bonsai is often practised. This involves artificially dwarfing otherwise large trees or shrubs, so as to give them an appearance of being stunted by wind and restricted root growth. (This is naturally seen when a seedling has been growing on a mountainside for decades and has become tortured and stunted due to the conditions.)

There are many places to purchase bonsai plants, but they tend to be very expensive, due to the amount of time spent creating them. Almost any shrub or tree can be made to look like a bonsai, by keeping the roots restricted and by selective pruning of certain branches and stems and wiring branches so they can be twisted into their desired shape.

The main disadvantage to this kind of scheme is that the plants need much more regular watering, as the pots they are grown in are usually shallow and become full of roots.

So, remember not to let them dry out and to give shelter from the strong winds (especially in spring with the fresh foliage). A wooden slatted shelter will protect bonsai from sun and wind.

Materials

- *Terracotta pots* These are very common sights in Spain and Portugal, in fact you often see plants growing in rusty old tin cans and buckets, so anything goes! Paint old containers in bright colours. It's also worth remembering that imitation plastic terracotta is much lighter and cheaper than the real thing.
- *Clay or terracotta drainage pipes* These are excellent receptacles for planting. Stood upright and filled with soil, most low, bushy plants can grow happily in them.
- *Gravel* As with the oriental style, gravel works well around pots and as a general floor covering.
- *Silver sand* This is the sand used in children's sandpits, and really adds to the theme. It can be used to complement the terracotta and Mediterranean plants.
- *Wooden chairs* These can look very effective painted light blue.

Tips

- The compost for all these plants should be fairly sandy and well drained. Ensure that all containers have adequate drainage holes so as to prevent waterlogging in winter which rots the roots.
- Troughs of brightly coloured trailing geraniums are very much in keeping with this type of scene, and will give a mass of colour for many months in the summer.
- Regular trimming of silver-leaved plants and herbs in spring and summer will keep them bushy and compact.

OTHER THEMES

Cottage garden

Use plants usually associated with small village gardens. This is great for summer colour but fairly dull in winter. You will need plenty of time to maintain this type of garden, which is always important to remember when choosing your particular style of roof garden.

Tropical garden

Choose plants for their lush jungle-like foliage. Obviously they have to be hardy, so careful choices must be made. Some of the plants we use in the makeover Malaysian garden fall into this category (see page 123).

Self-contained water features are also needed to give that very important sound of moving water and jungle stream impression.

PLANTINGS FOR ROOF GARDENS

Almost any type of plant can be used on a roof garden as long as certain cultivation rules are followed. Even fruit and vegetables do very well, and the ornamental types look particularly good.

The most important aspect is the compost. I would always use a loam-based compost, as the extra weight may help against any wind destabilizing the plants. Also this compost tends to hold moisture better in drying conditions.

Clipped box are easy to grow and add formality to this suburban roof garden.

With the addition of water-retention granules to the compost, longer periods of drought will be tolerated. The granules swell up and store water for the plants to use later.

- Use loam-based compost with water-retention granules, ericaceous compost for acid-loving plants.
- Some plants may need watering every day in hot sunny weather. Remember to water even in winter about once a fortnight.
- Choose plants that are wind- and sun-resistant.

ANNUALS

Most annuals will be fine on a roof garden. If it is very sunny and exposed, they will need watering frequently in the summer. It may be easiest to use an automatic watering system, especially if you are out a lot or are going on holiday (see page 112).

CONIFERS

Never let conifers get dry in summer or winter, as they will suffer from wind-burn more easily.

- *Abies koreana* (Korean fir). Soft green foliage; conical habit; blue-purple cones in autumn to winter; hardy; in pot approx. 1.5 m × 90 cm (5 × 3 ft) in 10 years.
- *Cryptomeria japonica* (Japanese cedar). (Lush limey-green foliage in summer and bronzy-red in winter; in pot approx. 1.5 m × 90 cm (5 × 3 ft) in 10 years.

- Juniperus (juniper). Usually low-growing, tough plants, tolerant of dryness, wind and cold; various colours; many different growth rates; *J. squamata* 'Blue Star' reaches only 45 × 45 cm (18 × 18 in) in 10 years; (see page 29 and 75).
- *Picea glauca* var. *albertiana* 'Conica'. (See page 29); 75 × 45 cm (30 × 18 in) in 10 years.
- *Picea pungens* 'Globosa'. (See page 29); 30 × 45 cm (12 × 18 in) in 10 years.
- *Pinus mugo* 'Mops'. (See page 29); 30 × 30 cm (12 × 12 in) in 10 years.
- *Pinus parviflora* 'Templehof'. Upright habit; blue-grey foliage; hardy; cones when older; in pot approx. 1.2 m × 45 cm (4 ft × 18 in) in 10 years.
- *Chamaecyparis thyoïdes* 'Andelyensis'. Lush green in summer, but changes to purplish in winter; very slow, upright growth; hardy; 60 × 30 cm (2 ft × 12 in) in 10 years.
- *Thuja occidentalis* 'Rheingold'. Golden-yellow foliage, a coppery orange in winter; conical habit; hardy; in pot approx. 90 × 60 cm (3 × 2 ft) in 10 years.

EVERGREEN SHRUBS

- *Camellia japonica*. (See page 42.)
- *Fatsia japonica* (caster oil plant). (See page 42); in pot approx. 90 × 90 cm (3 × 3 ft) in 10 years.
- *Mahonia japonica*. (See page 43); in pot approx. 1.2 m × 90 cm (4 × 3 ft) in 10 years.
- *Pieris japonica*. (See page 43); in pot approx. 90 × 90 cm (3 × 3 ft) in 10 years.

RHODODENDRONS

A huge family of plants which will look great all year round. Here are some of my favourite dwarf varieties.

- *Rhododendron* × *cilpinense*. Very early pale pink flowers; very unusual, open, tortured habit with peeling bark and a coloured trunk; looks like a bonsai; in pot approx. 75 × 45 cm (30 × 18 in).
- *Rhododendron* 'Blue Diamond'. Very dwarf type with tiny leaves and lavender flowers; scented foliage; very hardy; in pot approx. 45 × 45 cm (18 × 18 in) in 10 years.
- *Rhododendron yakushimanum*. A beautiful species with a compact habit, comes in a variety of flower colours and unusual browny 'fur' on the underside of the leaves; in pot approx. 45 × 60 cm (18 × 24 in) in 10 years.

DECIDUOUS SHRUBS

Losing leaves in the winter may not be a disadvantage, especially if the roof garden is not being used much at that time of year. Many deciduous shrubs have wonderful autumn colours and others have beautiful flowers.

- Acer (Japanese maples). All can do well on roof gardens as long as they are sheltered from cold winds and the drying sun.
- *Acer palmatum* 'Osakazuki'. Has one of the most striking autumn colours of all Japanese maples; its upright, spreading habit, makes it the ideal acer for a taller specimen on the roof garden; in pot approx. 1.2 m × 90 cm (4 × 3 ft) in 10 years.
- *Acer shirasawanum* f. *aureum*. Probably one of the slowest growing maples; beautiful, soft, golden-yellow leaves, upright habit; needs wind and sun protection; in pot approx. 60 × 30 cm (2 ft × 12 in) in 10 years.
- *Cotoneaster horizontalis*. If grown in a pot, these plants will grow horizontally and will form beautiful, layered growth; with careful pruning, a real bonsai effect can be achieved; very hardy with bright red berries, noticeable when the rich autumn coloured foliage has fallen off. Prune to any size.

CLIMBERS AND WALL SHRUBS

See chapter The Shady Garden for suggestions of climbers which tolerate shade.

- Ceanothus (Californian lilac). Powder blue flowers smothering stems in early summer; evergreen; not good for a very cold, exposed site. Needs sun.
- Clematis. Most varieties are good as long as the root area is shaded.
- *Fremontodendron* 'California Glory'. Silvery evergreen foliage tolerant of drought; huge yellow flowers over many months in summer.
- *Jasminum officinalis* (summer jasmine). Vigorous climber with pure white, richly scented flowers for many months.
- Lonicera (honeysuckle). Most honeysuckles will be fine; *L. japonica* 'Halliana' is my favourite as it is evergreen and bears creamy yellow scented flowers over a long period.

HEDGING PLANTS

There are a few useful hedging plants for roof gardens that are hardy and relatively quick growing. All can be grown in troughs as long as they are kept well watered and fed in summer.

- *Cotoneaster franchetii.* Semi-evergreen, with small, dark green leaves and upright habit; white flowers in early summer, followed by attractive berries.
- *Escallonia* 'Apple Blossom'. Shiny, evergreen leaves, lovely pink flowers in early summer.
- *Ligustrum ovalifolium* 'Aureum' (golden privet). Bright and cheerful foliage; tough, easy to grow; white flowers if not pruned.
- *Pyracantha* 'Orange Glow'. Tough, evergreen with beautiful white flowers, followed by orange-red berries which last well into winter; best tied up to railings or trellis.
- *Taxus baccata* (yew). Quite slow-growing initially, but easy to train and very tough.
- *Thuja occidentalis* 'Smaragd'. This deep-green conifer grows upright and narrow, ideal for this purpose.

ORIENTAL THEME

Choosing plants for containers that will give you the oriental 'feel' is open to interpretation. I have often used certain shrubs and conifers that look perfect in this environment, but are maybe from the Mediterranean, for instance!

Don't waste your time on tender plants, unless you can give them special shelter in winter. Watering must be a main concern, so select plants that can tolerate drought if you haven't the time to spend caring for them every day.

Here are my favourite conifers and shrubs for the oriental theme that never fail to please:

Conifers

- *Cedrus deodara* 'Golden Horizon' (golden cedar). Beautiful, bright golden yellow new growth; horizontal habit when young; hardy; if kept in pot, height in 10 years will be 60–90 cm (2–3 ft), spread 60–90 cm (2–3 ft).
- *Chamaecyparis obtusa* 'Nana Gracilis'. Twisted sprays of deep green foliage, resembling a bonsai; hardy; if kept in pot, height in 10 years will be 60–90 cm (2–3 ft), spread 60–90 cm (2–3 ft).
- *Pinus* (pine). Most species are ideal; even the taller-growing specimens are fine, as constriction in a container will reduce its speed of growth.
- *Pinus strobus* 'Nana'. Soft blue-green foliage, rounded habit; attractive cones in autumn to winter; if kept in pot, height in 10 years will be 60–90 cm (2–3 ft), spread 60–90 cm (2–3 ft).
- *Pinus* var. *mughus* (mountain pine). Slow-growing, very hardy pine with low habit; cones when older; if kept in pot, height in 10 years will be 60–90 cm (2–3 ft), spread 60–90 cm (2–3 ft).

Shrubs

- *Acer palmatum* 'Dissectum'. Delicately serrated light green leaves which turn bronze and scarlet in autumn; low-spreading habit; if kept in pot, height in 10 years will reach 60–90 cm (2–3 ft), spread to 60–90 cm (2–3 ft).

• *Acer palmatum* 'Dissectum Garnet'. Similar in habit to 'Dissectum', but has deep, wine-red foliage through summer and bronze-red autumn tints; if kept in pot, height in 10 years will reach 60–90 cm (2–3 ft), spread to 60–90 cm (2–3 ft).

• *Aralia elata* (devil's walking stick). Spiny stems give this plant its common name; variegated forms are much slower growing, but their size makes them more suitable to this type of confined space; if in pot, height in 10 years will reach 1.2–1.5 m (4–5 ft), spread to 1.2–1.5 m (4–5 ft).

• Azalea *(Rhododendron japonicum)* (Japanese azalea). Deep green foliage; flowers spring–early summer are white, pink, red, mauve or purple; needs lime-free compost, keep moist; if kept in pot, height in 10 years will be 60–90 cm (2–3 ft), spread 60–90 cm (2–3 ft).

• Bamboo (such as *Arundinaria*). Evergreen, but may look a bit untidy in winter, especially in an exposed situation; many dwarf varieties; need plenty of water; some grow to 60 cm (2 ft), others to 2 m (7 ft).

• *Euonymus alatus* (spindle tree). Unusual shrub with small, pale green leaves which turn a brilliant shade of glowing pink in autumn; stems are also interesting in winter; if kept in pot, height in 10 years will reach 60–90 cm (2–3 ft), spread to 60–90 cm (2–3 ft).

• *Rhododendron* 'Praecox'. One of the first to flower in early spring; deep mauve blossoms fading to a much lighter shade; open habit; if kept in pot, height in 10 years will reach 60–90 cm (2–3 ft), spread to 60 cm (2 ft).

MEDITERRANEAN THEME

Plants that normally grow in hot, dry conditions such as the Mediterranean, are well equipped to tolerate life on the roof garden. Silvery leaved species are ideal, and often have aromatic foliage and attractive flowers. Spiky leaved plants are also perfect in this theme. Not only do they look striking but they need minimal moisture.

Annual flowers such as Livingstone daisies and portulacas give a bright, gaudy display throughout the summer period. They fit in perfectly here and their fleshy, succulent leaves help them to survive drought conditions.

Here are some suitable fool-proof plants:

• Artemisia (see page 72).
• *Berberis thunbergii* 'Atropurpurea Nana' (see page 28).
• *Berberis* × *stenophylla* 'Irwinii' (see page 28).
• Caryopteris (see page 28).
• *Ceanothus repens* (see page 73).
• Cistus (rock rose) (see page 14).
• *Euonymus radicans*. Evergreen, very robust; variegated foliage, gold or silvery.
• Fuchsia (see page 15).
• *Genista lydia* (see page 28).
• Hebe (see page 28 and 74).
• Lavender (see page 28 and 74).
• Pittosporum. Beautiful evergreen shrubs, often with variegated leaves; need to be a little sheltered from icy winds in winter.
• Sage (see page 73).
• Yucca. Spiky leaves make this an excellent specimen plant; white flower spikes appear in late summer.

The Malaysian Roof Garden

olia and Rick had moved into the premises of a run-down pub near the city centre. They had decided to convert the downstairs into a restaurant, which was proving hard work and left them little time or space for themselves. The pub had a large but bare and inhospitable roof area which was sturdy enough for some serious improvement. They hoped to make an area both for entertainment and for relaxation where they could escape the hustle and bustle of the restaurant. Nolia wanted a Malaysian theme to remind her of home, with plenty of lush foliage.

A barren roof seems an impossible place to transform.

Design

The roof garden was big enough for me to be a little self-indulgent. There was a large lime tree which came up from next door's garden giving a solid background.

Nolia agreed it would be lovely to have a Malaysian-style hut here, and she was willing to let me try out an unusual idea: a painted pond-shape, using light blue pond-sealer, dressed up to give the impression of water!

The programme schedule meant that we had to complete the makeover in just one day. Although I did not want to cut corners, budget was high on the list of priorities, so where possible, cheap, readily available materials were used.

Materials

20 × 25 kg (55 lb) bags of 'oatmeal' ornamental gravel
6 × 25 kg (55 lb) flat slate cobbles
3 × 'Literock' artificial rockery stones
11 × Apta Malaysian pots
1 × wooden bridge
1 × 1 litre (2 pints) Pondseal paint
8 × bundles Norfolk reed

Malaysian hut

8 × 2.5 m (8 ft) heavy rustic poles
8 × 1.8 m (6 ft) heavy rustic poles
4 × 1.8 × 1.5 m (6 × 5 ft) bamboo screens
11 × 3 m × 15 cm × 2.5 cm (10 ft × 6 in × 1 in) gravel boards
nails and plastic-coated wire

Step-by-step

1 **Getting materials up on the roof**
Materials and plants were delivered to the site. A local scissor-lift firm agreed to help and saved us innumerable trips up and down four flights of stairs.

2 **Preparation** We then cleared the site of rubbish and debris using the lift to take down any unwanted material and swept it thoroughly.

3 **Building the hut** We decided to use rustic timbers for the main framework to give a natural effect.

Two uprights for the back of the building were nailed to one horizontal beam at the top (roof level), and one set 30 cm (1 ft) up from ground, to form a rectangle. The same thing was done to the front two uprights and horizontals. The front frame was 45 cm (18 in) lower than the back, to give us a forward-sloping roof: high at the back, low at the front. Connecting poles were then nailed from the front to the back sections on both ends, to hold the main framework together.

Next, 3-m (10-ft) gravel boards were fixed 30 cm (1 ft) off the ground, which made the floor of the building and strengthened the whole thing. Two more legs were fixed between the two outer ones, and this gave a Malaysian house-on-stilts effect.

With two further posts supporting the roof, we fixed on our bamboo roof: two thin bamboo screens were used as the roof, nailed and wired down to the framework. Two more bamboo screens were used to enclose the building and give privacy, especially in winter when the large lime tree had lost its foliage.

To add the finishing touches to our 'traditional hut', we used Norfolk reed as final decoration. This was simply tied in small bundles and then fixed to the bamboo screens, adding character and bulk to the rather thin, flat back wall and roof.

The legs of the hut were screwed to steel angle brackets which were then bolted to the solid roof surface.

The final interior floor space ended up about 3 m × 1.2 m (10 × 4 ft), enough for two to three people to sit comfortably and shelter from the mid-day sun (or rain). The back height was about 2.4 m (8 ft), the front 1.95 m (6 ft). Because the floor was raised by 30 cm (1 ft), tall people had to bend to get in, which actually made it more cosy.

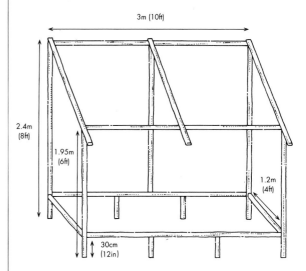

4 **The pond** The size and shape of the pond was marked out with a piece of rope. The surface was cleaned before painting started. We used Lotus Pondseal for the paint, which is normally used to waterproof concrete ponds. The effect was quite striking even without further dressing-up.

When it had dried, we dressed the pool edge with river-eroded slate pebbles. These disguised the edge and gave the illusion that the 'water' was at a lower level. To finish the overall effect, a small hump-backed wooden bridge was simply placed over the middle of the 'pond'.

5 **Planting** The plants I chose for Nolia's roof were obviously not strictly of Malaysian origin, but gave the impression of a lush, verdant garden. All were very hardy, despite having a tropical feel.

We transplanted the shrubs into Malaysian glazed pots, ensuring there was enough fresh compost around the existing rootball to suit the plant's needs.

Once repotted, the shrubs were moved around the garden until their ideal position was found. This process involved standing back and viewing from various angles. A flowering hibiscus finished off the planting – particularly pleasing as it is the Malaysian national flower! Nolia also painted hibiscus flowers on the chimney wall.

A painted pond gives a convincing impression when used with this hump-backed bridge and pebbles.

6 **Stepping stones and gravel** Wooden stepping stones were used to lead across the garden. The timber linked the wooden hut with the bridge, and made walking easier than on gravel alone. The stepping stones were fixed to the roof with a strong bonding compound.

The gravel very quickly hid the stark-looking tar roof, and added a rich and varied texture. Mixed, coloured gravel was used, giving more interest than one colour.

THE PLANTS USED FOR THE TV GARDEN

- 1 × *Aralia elata* (devil's walking stick) (see page 119).
- 1 × *Arundinaria murieliae* (bamboo). Hardy, tall-growing.
- 1 × *Arundaria pumila* 'Variegata'. Dwarf variegated bamboo; 60–90 cm (2–3 ft) high.
- 2 × *Decaisnea fargesii*. Tropical-looking foliage; beautiful blue seed pods in autumn-winter; 1.5–1.8 m (5–6 ft).
- 1 × *Hibiscus syriacus*. Needs sunny spot; beautiful flowers late summer; hardy; 90 cm–1.2 m (3–4 ft).
- 1 × *Rhus typhina* (now *R. hirta*) (stag's horn sumach). Normally grows into large shrub/tree; contained in pot it makes a lush foliage plant, with rich orange-red tints in autumn; 1.5–1.8 m (5–6 ft).
- 6 × *Rhus hirta* 'Laciniata'. Slower growing with beautiful dissected leaves.
- 8 × Canna lilies. Ideal flowers to give a real splash of vivid colour; tropical-looking foliage gives a banana-plant appearance.

Useful Addresses

THE PATIO GARDEN

Plants supplied by
Wyevale Garden Centres PLC,
Kings Acre Road, Hereford HR4 0SE.
Ring (01432) 276568 for nearest branch

Old Weatherdale paving supplied by
Bradstones, Hulland Ward, Ashbourne,
Derbyshire DE6 3ET Tel: (0335) 372222

Water feature supplied by
Wildwoods Water Gardens Ltd,
Theobalds Park Road, Crews Hill, Enfield,
Middx EN2 9BP. Tel: (0181) 366 0243

Medallion turf supplied by
Rolawn Turf Ltd, Elvington,
York YO4 5AR. Tel: (0904) 608661

THE ROCK GARDEN

Plants and materials supplied by
Fulmer Plant Park, Cherry Tree Lane,
Fulmer, Bucks, SL8 6JE. Tel: (01753) 663367

THE SHADY GARDEN

Plants supplied by
Blakedown Nurseries Ltd,
Belbroughton Road, Blakedown,
Kidderminster, Worcestershire DY10 3JG.
Tel: (01562) 700551.

Tree ferns supplied by
Hanging Garden Nurseries,
Tytherleigh House, Hubert Road, Brentwood,
Essex CM14 4RF. Tel: (01277) 227606

Materials supplied by
Lewis Tyler and Sons, Estate Sawmill,
Mill Green, Hatfield AL9 5PG.
Tel: (01707) 268523

THE WATER GARDEN

Plants and materials supplied by
Wildwoods Water Gardens Ltd,
Theobalds Park Road, Crews Hill, Enfield,
Middx EN2 9BP. Tel: (0181) 366 0243

THE LOW-MAINTENANCE GARDEN

Plants and materials supplied by
The Dutch Nursery, Bell Bar, Hatfield.
Tel: (01707) 653372

THE NEGLECTED GARDEN

Plants supplied by
The Dutch Nursery (see above)

THE FAMILY GARDEN

Medallion turf supplied by
Rolawn Turf Ltd, Elvington, York YO4 5AR.
Tel: (0904) 608661

Plants and pergola supplied by
The Dutch Nursery (see above)

THE ROOF GARDEN

Fake pond materials supplied by
Wildwoods Water Gardens Ltd,
Theobalds Park Road, Crews Hill, Enfield,
Middx EN2 9BP. Tel: (0181) 366 0243

Pots supplied by
APTA Pottery, J1 Dencora Way,
Leacon Road, Fairwood Business Park,
Ashford, Kent TN23 4FH. Tel: (0233) 621090

Plants and hut supplied by
The Dutch Nursery (see above)

PICTURE CREDITS

MIRACLE MAKEOVERS WITH THE GARDEN GURU
BBC Books would like to thank the following for providing photographs and for permission to reproduce copyright material. While every effort has been made to trace and acknowledge all copyright holders, we would like to apologize should there have been any errors or omissions.

BBC Books pages 18, 19, 30, 31, 47, 49, 62, 63, 78, 79, 91, 93, 103, 105, 122 (Anne Hyde), page 59 (John Jefford); **The Garden Picture Library** pages 11, 14–15, 22, 27, 34, 39, 43, 50, 54, 66, 67, 71, 83, 86, 87, 95, 99, 106, 110–111, 115; **Jerry Harpur** page 98; **Antony Henn** pages 46, 102; **Photos Horticultural** pages 6, 26; **Gavin Rota** pages 16, 61, 77, 90, 120.

Index